MISSION IRAN

MISSION IRAN

Special Forces Berlin & Operation EAGLE CLAW
JTF 1-79

JAMES STEJSKAL

CASEMATE
Pennsylvania & Yorkshire

Published in the United States of America and Great Britain in 2024 by
CASEMATE PUBLISHERS
1950 Lawrence Road, Havertown, PA 19083
and
47 Church Street, Barnsley, S70 2AS, UK

Copyright 2024 © James Stejskal

Paperback Edition: ISBN 978-1-63624-333-7
Digital Edition: ISBN 978-1-63624-334-4

A CIP record for this book is available from the British Library

Printed and bound in the United Kingdom by CPI Group (UK) Ltd, Croydon, CR0 4YY

Typeset in India by Lapiz Digital Services, Chennai.

For a complete list of Casemate titles, please contact:

CASEMATE PUBLISHERS (US)
Telephone (610) 853-9131
Fax (610) 853-9146
Email: casemate@casematepublishers.com
www.casematepublishers.com

CASEMATE PUBLISHERS (UK)
Telephone (0)1226 734350
Email: casemate@casemateuk.com
www.casemateuk.com

Front cover images: Top image, OH-6 helicopter (public domain); bottom image, Iranian Foreign Affairs Ministry. (Wikimedia Commons)
Back cover image: Break between daylight live-fire rehearsals. (Author's photo)

Contents

This short history is dedicated to the men I served with in Detachment "A" Berlin, a.k.a. 39th Special Forces Detachment. It was the best of times and, occasionally, the worst of times, but we were the few, that band of brothers, and we held the line. As our comrade and friend "JJ" Morrison said, "It would have been glorious."

Introduction

Diplomats serving abroad for the United States are often confronted with difficult and dangerous tasks. Difficult because living conditions in some countries are less than optimal by the typical "American" standards. Dangerous because Americans are often targeted by terrorists, criminals, and even the government of the host country. That was certainly true in the late 1970s when revolutionaries overran the U.S. Embassy in Tehran, Iran, and took over fifty American diplomats prisoner on November 4, 1979, a hostage incident that lasted 444 days.

But the story did not start on that day. Its roots lie in the complicated relationship that had existed between the two countries since the early 1940s. The overthrow of Prime Minister Mohammad Mosaddegh through an army coup supported by the British and the U.S. governments reinstated Shah Mohammad Reza Pahlavi. Friendly to the United States, the Shah guaranteed a steady supply of oil in return for economic and military aid. But, as with most despots, the Shah refused to permit political freedom.

His regime was condemned by Iranian nationalists who saw the United States as the real power behind the Peacock Throne. Riots in 1963 led to suppression of the opposition and crackdowns against anyone seen as a threat to the government. Arrests were numerous, and the Shah's SAVAK (the intelligence and security organization of Iran) gained a reputation for ruthlessness and brutality. Among those arrested was the religious leader Ayatollah Ruhollah Khomeini, a bitter foe of the United States, who was later exiled to France.

Between 1963 and 1979, the Shah spent the majority of Iran's budget on weapons and failed to promote economic progress or expand democratic freedoms. A disgruntled populace resorted to revolution. With the government nearing collapse, the Shah fled the country on January 16, 1979.

Khomeini returned to Tehran in February 1979 to lead a new government and immediately launched into a campaign of vitriol against the Great Satan—the United States of America. When U.S. President Jimmy Carter permitted the Shah to travel to the United States for medical treatment in August 1979, the Ayatollah stepped up his rhetoric, and protests against the U.S. started to take an ominous turn. By November, political dynamics in Iran and the international arena reached a fever pitch. Khomeini's supporters turned to violence to drive opposition parties from their government positions and consolidate complete control, while he demanded the Shah's extradition back to Iran for trial.

On November 4, 1979, "student" supporters of the Ayatollah seized the U.S. Embassy with over sixty hostages.[1] Relations between the two countries headed south. It was a situation never before experienced in American diplomacy. Europeans had been touched by international terrorism since the late 1960s, but for most Americans, the Iran Hostage Crisis was a watershed. It was one of the first times America felt terrorism so directly and on such a large scale.

The Cold War was in full swing and the United States had only begun to fight international terrorism, only begun to understand the tactics of terror that are now all too familiar. The learning curve, both political and military, has been steep and often deadly.

What follows is one piece of that history.

CHAPTER I

A Short History of Detachment "A" Berlin (39th Special Forces Detachment)

When Nazi Germany fell at the end of World War II, its capital Berlin quickly became a point of contention between the Soviets and the Western Allies of the United States, Britain, and France. At the Yalta Conference, these Allies finalized their agreement to divide Germany into zones of occupation. The Americans, British, and French occupied what would be known as West Germany, while the Soviets occupied East Germany. Deep inside the Soviet zone, Berlin was similarly divided into four zones of occupation. Although the Allies had small numbers of troops in Berlin compared to the East German and Soviet forces that surrounded the city, they were prepared to defend the city. Although the small Allied occupation army in Berlin would be little more than an annoyance to the massive Group of Soviet Forces in Germany, it could serve as a delaying force to slow their advance.

A relative newcomer to the world, the U.S. Army Special Forces was established in 1952, the brainchild of several veterans of World War II. Its progenitor was the Office of Strategic Services (OSS), a unique organization that was responsible for espionage, sabotage, and other forms of unconventional warfare (UW). When the OSS was disbanded in 1945, the conventionally minded Army saw no need for UW and chose not to replace its capabilities. Others disagreed with that assessment, including General Robert McClure, who ran psychological warfare operations for General Eisenhower, and Colonels Aaron Bank, Wendell Fertig, and Russell Volckmann, all of whom had run guerrilla operations against the Axis during the war. Together they realized the U.S. military needed the

UW capability, and they convinced the Joint Chiefs of Staff to form the first unit of its kind in the U.S. Army, the 10th Special Forces Group (Airborne). The 853 men of the 10th deployed to Bad Tölz, Germany, in the fall of 1953.

Detachment "A" was established in the summer of 1956 in response to a request by the Commander of U.S. Forces in Berlin (USCOB) to provide him with "demolition squads" to destroy strategic targets outside the city. Plans were made to assign six U.S. Army Special Forces (SF) "A" teams to Berlin Command who were to assist with harassing and delaying any Soviet advance toward West Germany in the event of war. Six teams were secretly deployed from Bad Tölz in Berlin to form the unit and were stationed at the former Telefunken Factory complex and ostensibly assigned to Headquarters, 6th Infantry Regiment; they would be known as the "Security Platoon." In April 1958, the unit moved again, this time several kilometers across town to Andrews Barracks, where it was hidden within the Headquarters and Headquarters Company of U.S. Army Garrison Berlin.[1] It was a location that would permit expansion and better security. The unit was renamed Detachment "A" and was simply called the Detachment, or Det "A" for short. In official planning documents the unit was referred to as "Special Forces Berlin" and was officially designated as the 39th Special Forces Detachment on August 27, 1965.[2]

Unconventional Warfare Experts

The 39th's classified mission was that "upon the outbreak of general hostilities or under certain conditions of localized war," the teams would destroy targets inside the city of Berlin and nearby East Germany selected by the USCOB as vital to his successful defense of the city, as well as priority targets in the U.S. European Command (EUCOM) Unconventional War Plan. Once that tasking was completed, the teams would conduct UW operations as directed by Commander, Support Operations Task Force Europe (SOTFE). The concept was for each team to link up with local guerrilla forces and to assist them to organize, train, and fight the Soviet forces. It was an ambitious and extremely dangerous mission; some would call it suicidal.[3]

The unit operated under a light cover of "supporting the mission of the Berlin Brigade," without much more depth than not revealing the presence and true status of a Special Forces unit. The men all spoke German or at least one Eastern European language. Essentially, the unit members had to live three covers. The first was as a member of an army unit assigned to Berlin, including wearing a uniform, carrying an ID card, and the usual protocol that went with that. The second was as a civilian living in Berlin, including a U.S. civilian ID, civilian clothing, with a story like student, tradesman, barkeeper, medical field—whatever their background would support. And the third was reserved for war—foreign identity cards and a suitable cover. In that case—given civilian identity cards and non-U.S. passports—it was expected they would be able to operate clandestinely when and if war with the Warsaw Pact began. Day-to-day training included everything from weapons marksmanship, explosives, radio communications, and identification of Soviet uniforms, equipment, and units, to more esoteric subjects such as intelligence tradecraft, surreptitious methods of entry, disguises, cell organization, and caches.

While no other special operations-type unit was practicing this kind of operation at the time, Detachment "A" was employing it on a daily basis; something called Urban Unconventional Warfare. Special Forces' progenitor, the Office of Strategic Services or OSS, had trained on and used similar tactics and methods—collectively known as intelligence tradecraft—during World War II, skills passed on to its replacement, the Central Intelligence Agency. Due to the nature of the counterinsurgency war in Vietnam, the U.S. Army Special Forces had distanced itself for the most part from the "urban" portion of these activities, which—at the most basic level—were the same skills intelligence agencies used to conduct clandestine agent operations. These skills include conducting surveillance of targets and individuals, counter surveillance—sometimes called surveillance detection—agent handling operations, and technical and non-technical communications. Communications in an enemy-controlled urban area are not only crucial but dangerous as well. Technical communications required the unit's operators—either alone or as a member of a team—to use HF (high frequency) radios in an urban area. This was no easy task when you had to conceal a fifty to a hundred-foot-long wire antenna and send messages quickly to prevent enemy radio direction finders from discovering your location. Non-technical communications are those methods used for operators and agents to maintain clandestine (hidden) contact. These include casing operations (the same skills used by criminals to "case" and rob a bank), dead letter drops (DLD or DD), brush passes (BP), brief encounters (BE), as well as the use of signal sites, codes, and secret writing—all very esoteric skills. These subjects were usually taught by former intelligence officers in the employ of what was euphemistically called the "other government agency" or OGA, including CIA instructors who worked under such codenames as "Team 10."

RED SAILS

Once their clandestine tradecraft skills were up to par, the unit's operators put them into practice in daily operations inside Berlin and elsewhere. That gave the unit a capability that no other special operations element in the U.S. military possessed. One specific training operation called "RED SAILS" illustrates why—it was a key reason the unit was chosen for the Iran rescue mission.

In early 1978, the Secret Intelligence Service (SIS), a.k.a. MI6, sought out assistance from the United States to train local British security forces in how to better identify and track terrorist teams that might try to carry out operations in the UK. Since the early 1970s, the Irish Republican Army (IRA) had successfully infiltrated small sabotage teams into mainland UK who would select a target, conduct surveillance, and then attack it with explosives or firearms. Up to that point a number of attacks had been carried out by the IRA, including bombings in London, Birmingham, and Bristol.

SIS wanted to use outside "specialists" to simulate a terrorist operation in order to make the training more realistic, as opposed to using the British SAS, who had the home-field advantage. The exercise would test British inter-service capabilities to track a terrorist team in and around Southampton, a large port city in the coastal region of southwestern England. The SIS/MI6 officers acted as exercise controllers, while MI5 and local police were the local security force that was learning from the exercise. But, as is often the case with America's British "cousins," there was a larger agenda.

When the request was received, SOTFE tasked Detachment "A" to conduct the exercise that was codenamed "RED SAILS." The first team to go consisted of four operators with extensive experience who initially thought they would teach terrorist modus operandi to police officers. They were quickly disabused of that notion and told they were expected to act as terrorists themselves and were given several missions to accomplish. They would be a clandestine red team to test British security procedures while law enforcement tried to catch them in the act.

With that, the team realized the game was stacked against them. Their rental car, hotel rooms, even the targets they were to notionally attack had been chosen by their hosts. There was only one thing to do, so they changed the game, abandoned everything they had been provided with, and made new arrangements, effectively disappearing from the scene.

They had prepared for eventualities, however, primarily because no one trusted either the American command which gave them this "training tasking" or their British cousins who were never beyond changing the rules to fit their needs. The one thing they couldn't change was the targets the controllers chose for the Americans to reconnoiter, locations similar to what terrorists would have also selected, such as police stations and electrical transformer yards. The team decided to use their best tradecraft—no public meetings, only clandestine messages passed through dead drops—to accomplish their tasks. Their approaches to the targets were carefully choreographed to avoid the British surveillance they knew would be watching for them.

Going underground meant they often had to sleep rough—away from hotels and conveniences. Several of the team made contact with old friends who were easily persuaded to join in the "games." Non-technical communications were used to eliminate the dangers of open telephone lines—dead drops and brief encounters made passing messages more cumbersome and less timely, but it was secure.

Occasional missteps had to be dealt with as well. One operator was compromised when his hidden handheld radio was discovered in the flophouse room he had rented. The owner was a retired police constable and quickly reported the man to authorities. He was promptly arrested. The British tried to play him back against his teammates by calling for an emergency meeting, but the safety codewords needed to authenticate the message were left out by the arrested (and very chagrined) operator. The meeting went down, but not as the police expected. A young Briton who had been enticed by a reward delivered a butcher-wrapped package of pig offal to the meeting. He was detained and questioned without revealing any information, and the three remaining team members were able to complete their sabotage tasks successfully.

Two subsequent versions of RED SAILS were run after MI6 decided the exercise was better run as an unscripted game, which allowed the Americans even more advantages. Such were the results that the British sent a letter to the commander of Detachment "A" that requested the team be seconded to the SIS for service in Northern Ireland. All along, it seems, the exercises were intended to see if the Americans were suitable to infiltrate the IRA in Northern Ireland. Apparently, they were.

Counterterrorism

The unit had operated under its single tasking of unconventional warfare until 1975, when it was assigned a secondary mission of counterterrorism (CT) under U.S. Army Europe Concept of Operations Plan 0300 (USAREUR CONPLAN 0300). The first order of business was to train for the current threat: aircraft hijackings. In 1974, Detachment "A" had been assigned the responsibility for providing sniper support to the Berlin Brigade in the event an American aircraft was hijacked in Berlin. As Berlin was still under Allied occupation, any hijacking or terrorism problem in the city fell under the Allied jurisdiction, and all aircraft that landed in West Berlin belonged either to Pan Am, British Airways, Air France, or their subsidiaries.

The unit's first external CT training began with the FBI. Using the general requirement to support the Brigade, Det "A"'s commander, Lieutenant Colonel Sidney Shacknow, coordinated the attendance of six members of Det "A" at a special FBI Anti-Air Crimes course in the spring of 1974. The six included Captain Mercer "Mac" Dorsey, Lieutenant Grayal Farr, Sergeant First Class John Niffenegger, Staff Sergeant Kevin Monahan, Sergeant First Class Donald Airhart, and Captain Richard LaHue. Along with the FBI agents undergoing the training, several Canadian Mounted Police officers, two German Federal Intelligence Service (BND) officers, and a team of German Federal Border Protection Group 9 (GSG-9) officers, including their commander, Colonel Ulrich Wegener, attended the course.

Grayal Farr later recounted the training:

> When we assumed the counter-skyjacking mission we asked around for training. The FBI had a lot of skyjacking experience by that time and had the best possible scenarios and facilities (an actual DC 8, FBI former airline pilots, air controllers, and stewardesses as role-players) so it was exactly what we needed to begin with.
>
> A team of six personnel was sent to Quantico for a "custom-tailored" air crimes training course. There were other "outsiders" there at the same time including a team from GSG-9, who made a lousy impression during the course. They did not want to exert themselves physically giving the impression they were above the drudgery of actual training.
>
> In my day airline "security" consisted of having passengers identify their bags as they boarded the aircraft. That was a big innovation and assumed to be certain insurance against on-boarding bombs. The FBI training did not include any CQB-type [Close-Quarter Battle] action. The FBI Special Weapons and Tactics (SWAT) teams with whom we trained were really up-gunned after their own SWAT qualification. From .38 revolvers to .357 revolvers—rapid reloads were accomplished with loose rounds from your pocket.[4]
>
> The GSG-9 guys were all impressive, SS recruiting poster-looking guys, whereas the BND officers were sort of nondescript. Colonel Wegener gave a great slide show about GSG-9 training and equipment. After the briefing our FBI host asked to hear about the Munich Olympic disaster, which Wegener had "witnessed" as the Aide de Camp to the Federal Interior Minister. Wegener refused. The FBI guy politely reminded him that everyone there was there expressly to learn how to deal with possible similar threats, such as the coming Olympics in Canada. Wegener simply said, "No dice."
>
> The two-week SWAT training focused on team building, getting FBI agents, accustomed to working alone or in pairs, to operate as a small tactical unit. The GSG guys treated the BND pair (who actually did as well or better at everything than the GSGs) like they were not in any sense part of the same team. The GSG-9 guys also opted out of specific events, notably the PT, which often included team combatives. In one such incident we ran two or three miles to complete a Marine obstacle course and ran back (timed by team finishes) and convened

in the gym. That day we had "Lions and Tigers." Two teams at a time were outfitted with helmets, crotch protectors, and boxing gloves. Teams sat back to back. When a whistle blew the object was to throw opposing team members off the mat until only one team remained. Wegener listened and refused. "*Steht nicht in Dienstplan*," he said. "It's not on the training schedule." So the Germans stood and watched while the FBI guys, Mounties, and SF guys battered and threw each other around. And their demeanor suggested that they were thereby demonstrating their superiority.

Marksmanship was nothing special either. A couple of the Mounties were marksmanship trainers and I became the first trainee in some time to ring up a perfect score on the rifle-then-pistol, five-range station, moving target course. On that same course, one GSG-9 guy a couple of stations down began to miss. He got madder and madder and was acting more out-of-control, almost childish, until the FBI range safety officer halted the exercise. Wegener went out and chewed the guy's ass and we all eventually finished (two pistol shots at a rapidly moving close-in target) the course. Meanwhile the two BNDs had quietly been dinging targets as consistently as the Mounty marksmanship instructors and some SF guys and a bunch of FBI agents.

The results of that training were taken back to Berlin, where the training was continued with the help of Pan Am Airlines at Tegel International Airport. Teams trained on the active flight line, acting as ground crews and baggage handlers. Although they were met with some hostility from the German airport employees, once they understood the reasoning, their attitude toward the Americans changed dramatically. SF Berlin members were permitted to handle actual incoming and departing flights (with some supervision) during the day. At night, the teams moved to a secluded section of the airfield and practiced dynamic entry techniques on Pan Am's stable of Boeing 737 and 727 aircraft. Scenarios for full-on aircraft assaults were conducted, with role-players for the terrorists, passengers, and the crews, until every team was considered up to "standard," although no specific standards had yet been developed.[5] After each scenario was run, everyone—role-players and team members—would conduct a hot-wash debriefing to determine successes and deficiencies.

Organization

Detachment "A" was organized as a Special Forces "B" Team, a reinforced company with six 11-man "A" teams and support personnel. For the CT mission, the overall command structure was called the Special Action Force (SAF), while each "A" team was known as a Special Action Team (SAT). The teams were further organized as two four-man Assault Teams and a three-man Sniper/Spotter Team. Each section was led by the most experienced member, not necessarily the senior officer or non-commissioned officer. Standard unit firearms, including the Walther MPK submachine gun and the P-38 pistol,[6] were carried. The sniper teams were equipped with the M-21 and Remington 40-XB sniper rifles, and the Heckler & Koch HK-21 machine gun. There were also some "special weapons" available for certain requirements.

Training

Later, the unit's operations officer, Captain Peter Kelly, and its senior enlisted man, Sergeant Major Jeff Raker, both German expatriates, were able to arrange training with the German Border Police CT unit, *Bundesgrenzschutz Gruppe-9* (GSG-9), and the Berlin Police's SEK or *Sondereinsatzkommando.* The Germans gave new insights into useful tactics and techniques, but in many ways, they were less prepared than their guests, the men from Detachment "A." Being essentially police SWAT teams, they had little concept of or experience with unconventional warfare, especially tradecraft in an urban environment, or the use of heavier weapons. One of the skills Det "A" brought to the game was the ability to go undercover as an operational team, whereas most police officers were not at all prepared to undertake such missions.

It should be noted that a number of the unit's men had been formerly assigned to Military Assistance Command Vietnam's Studies and Observations Group (MACV-SOG), which carried out clandestine operations in Southeast Asia in the 1960s and early 1970s.

The Detachment also counted among its members a number of troops who had cross-trained with the British Special Air Service (SAS) and were critical to integrating advanced methods of Close-Quarter Battle (CQB). Many others had set up and trained American police departments in urban SWAT tactics. Additional weapons training was done at Fort Bragg with the short-lived "Blue Light" unit at the Mott

Lake Compound, with at least two teams attending the so-called Special Operations Training (SOT) prior to 1979.

Using techniques gained from these varied sources and experiences, Det "A" built up its skills during night and day with CQB training and precision marksmanship (sniper) training, as well as the take-down of targets from single rooms to multistory buildings, and "linear targets" such as aircraft, buses, and trains, and close-protection (bodyguard) operations. By 1977, the unit was certified as the USEUCOM counterterrorism force. In 1978, Colonel Charlie Beckwith visited the unit to acquire insight into unit tactics and training. He also visited GSG-9 and the SAS to gain inspiration for the training and organization of his new unit at Fort Bragg in the United States.[7]

Prior to the Iran Embassy hostage incident, Detachment "A" was called out for a number of terrorism-related events, including providing close-protection details to General Al Haig and General Frederick Kroesen following assassination attempts by German terrorist groups in 1978 and 1979.

But it was Tehran that brought the unit's talents into focus, a mix of urban unconventional warfare experience—intelligence tradecraft and special operations—which emphasized clandestine, low-visibility operations, with an operational capability that, although small, was unparalleled to any other in the United States.

FIRST ACT

RICE BOWL to EAGLE CLAW

CHAPTER 2

Where It Began: Tehran, November 4, 1979

The morning started out quietly at the embassy but quickly turned into what would be a 444-day-long nightmare for the United States. Radical Iranians had planned to demonstrate in front of the large American diplomatic compound in order to air their grievances against the Great Satan. But, instead, the siege morphed into an all-out assault as hundreds of students stormed over the walls and seized 66 Americans as their hostages. Ostensibly, their complaint against the United States was that Iran's former leader, Shah Mohammad Reza Pahlavi, had been allowed exile to seek medical care in the United States. Some diplomats believed the students were protesting the direction the revolution was taking and wanted to marginalize the moderates for the benefit of the clerics. The event shook the U.S. Government and military, as the new provisional government of the Islamic Republic of Iran seemingly could not or deliberately would not do anything to resolve the issue.

The Iranian Revolution started in the fall of 1977 with sporadic demonstrations by opponents of the Pahlavi regime. Shortly after the ouster of the Shah in January 1979 and his departure, Ayatollah Ruhollah Khomeini returned to the country to take control. Within days, Khomeini's people were in charge of the government and trying to consolidate their position at the expense of the moderates. Despite the United States's best efforts to work with the new government, including warning them of Iraq's imminent intention to attack Iran, the radicals wanted nothing to do with the United States. When President Carter gave in to pressure and allowed the Shah to seek medical treatment in the United States, the storm broke loose. Khomeini denounced Carter's decision and the United States, while criticizing moderates and secularists in his own government. Radical students, thus encouraged, stormed the U.S. Embassy, while the remaining moderates within Khomeini's government quickly resigned. Khomeini cleverly used the incident to complete his vision of a hardline Islamic theocracy.

President Jimmy Carter had few options. Only several months before, Ayatollah Khomeini had resolved a similar incident with his personal intervention. It initially seemed that might be the case with this takeover, but it soon became clear that the minister's power had been usurped by the radicals. The rhetoric became much more ominous as the radicals' leaders threatened to kill all the hostages should the United States intervene. When the crisis began to drag on, Carter chose economic sanctions over military action, but the hostages remained in their new "prison," the American Embassy compound in central Tehran.

While diplomatic measures were underway, the military immediately began contingency planning for a rescue mission. The task would be Herculean, as the hostages were in hostile territory far from the United States. Only once before had such a difficult mission been attempted, when American forces tried to rescue POWs from a North Vietnamese prison at Son Tay in November 1970. That mission was conducted by helicopter assault from bases in neighboring Thailand and required massive resources to undertake. The Iran mission offered a much more difficult problem, because Tehran lay far beyond the range of any available helicopter, and the target was in the middle of a large, potentially hostile city.

Initially, EUCOM placed several military units on alert, including the 1/10th Special Forces Group in Bad Tölz, Germany, and the 1/509th Parachute Infantry Regiment in Vicenza, Italy, for an emergency rescue, but the order was quickly rescinded as it became clear the mission was too complex for a simple solution. The national assets would be called upon to execute the operation.

Detachment "A" in Berlin had been exposed to the Iran issue already. Earlier, as Iran spiraled into the revolutionary abyss in 1978, EUCOM tasked the unit to prepare for a potential deployment to protect, remove, or destroy sensitive U.S. assets located within the soon-to-be Islamic Republic. This mission did not go forward and the Detachment wasn't deployed; however, its preparation and familiarity with the target country ensured it would be involved in the rescue mission planning, which commenced immediately after November 4, 1979.

When President Carter outlined his goals for the mission, it was clear that he wanted to proceed with the least intrusive option:

> We want it to be quick, incisive, surgical, no loss of American lives, not involve any other country, minimal suffering of the Iranian people themselves, to increase their reliance on imports, sure of success, and unpredictable.[1]

To throw an additional wrench in everyone's planning, the following point was made: "be ready to execute in ten days or less."

The military's plan would be extremely complex, but first, information was required to prepare for the operation. With the seizure of the embassy, most of the CIA's capabilities had been eliminated—or so they said. And, although some Agency officers could possibly enter Iran, few were trained to collect the tactical intelligence needed or support the mission when it began.[2]

By 1979, the CIA's Directorate of Operations (DO)—the team of men and women used overseas primarily to recruit agents, collect intelligence, and perform other clandestine tasks—was a shadow of its former self. Twin personnel reductions of nearly 40 percent under the short tutelage of Director James Schlesinger, appointed by President Nixon, and then by President Carter's CIA Director, Admiral Stansfield Turner, had decimated and demoralized the Agency. These actions bookended the Senate's Church Committee investigation and hearings that exposed operations and struck at the very core of the DO and the agency as a whole. Those events coupled with the seizure of the embassy left the CIA with few if any assets on the ground in Tehran or the country of Iran. The Agency was not operationally prepared to assist, but beyond that problem lay a distrust of the military. It would later become apparent that the CIA was withholding specific information that, if revealed, could have endangered those few assets it did have.

At the Pentagon, General James B. Vaught was selected to head up the mission's Joint Task Force. The planning phase, Operation RICE BOWL, began with a study of the mission requirements and selection of the forces needed. As commander and senior NCO of Det "A"—one of the only two certified U.S. counterterrorism units—Colonel Stanley Olchovik and Sergeant Major Raker traveled to the Pentagon for in the initial consultations with the Special Operations Division to integrate the unit into what would be called Joint Task Force 1-79 (JTF 1-79).

The Top Secret mission statement was simply stated but belied how difficult its goal would be:

> MISSION: Joint Task Force conducts Operations to rescue U.S. personnel held hostage in the American Embassy Compound, Tehran, Iran.[3]

The plan would be even more complex because Americans were held in two locations—the embassy chancery compound and the Iranian Ministry of Foreign Affairs (MFA). It was also apparent the CIA would not provide adequate intelligence support. A CIA liaison officer told Raker at the time that the Agency was in contact with only one of its assets and they were unsure who actually was controlling him.

DoD planners came to the conclusion that it would have to fill the deficit of ground intelligence assets itself. After scouring the DoD databases for Iranian-born military members, the search was expanded to look at what other assets were available. The fact that the Army would likely be doing much of its own intel work on the ground forced planners to look inward. Since the Detachment was already in the conversation, Olchovik was tasked to conduct the advanced reconnaissance of the targets. The Detachment was the U.S. military's only dual-capability unit, having counterterrorism and unconventional warfare as its primary missions, and had the trained men to take on the job.

Then came the second mission tasking for the Detachment. As the consultations progressed, Colonel Charlie Beckwith, who had remained at Fort Bragg with his unit, announced that "SoF" could handle only the assault of the embassy compound.[4] He would need all of his 90 men to conduct that operation, which required the breaching of the compound's walls and the search of a number of buildings, all while securing the outside perimeter to counter any Iranian security force response. "SoF" simply did not have the manpower to take on the second target. As soon as those words were spoken, Olchovik immediately pronounced: "We can handle it."

With that, Detachment "A" would not only be involved in collecting the intelligence necessary for planning and assisting the assault forces' infiltration into Tehran, but it would also rescue the three Americans at the Foreign Ministry. It would be a very busy winter.

The U.S. Chargé d'Affaires Bruce Laingen and two other embassy officers, Victor Tomseth and Mike Howland, were being detained at the Foreign Ministry, where they had an appointment when the embassy compound was stormed. Now they were "guests" of the Foreign Minister, who declined to let them depart.

Back in Berlin, Sergeant Major Raker began planning for the mission. Because of its location and the visibility of the American military—Warsaw Pact spies were prolific in the city—all preparations were conducted with operational security in mind. The first decision was that all training and exercise commitments would be unchanged and the teams participating would be kept intact. That meant the men for the mission would be chosen from the remaining teams that were uncommitted. But before that challenge was undertaken, there was the question of who would go on the advance reconnaissance mission.

CHAPTER 3

Clem & Scotty

Throughout history, when a military leader has wanted to know what danger he is facing to his front, he has called for a reconnaissance—that is: what kind of enemy, what terrain, and what hostile reception awaited him. The command in cavalry days was "scouts out." The commander of TF-179 faced the same dilemma. He didn't know what he needed to know. Almost immediately, the Pentagon saw that the national intelligence community would not be able to provide the tactical information it needed to plan and execute the mission to recover the American hostages. And almost as quickly, it realized that the American military did not have the properly trained personnel who could conduct a clandestine intelligence collection trip into Iran—with one exception: Detachment "A" Berlin.

In January 1980, Clem Lemke, the man called the "Mad German" by his comrades, had been called back to Berlin from Berchtesgaden where he had been conducting Alpine ski training with his team. He was met at the airport by Detachment "A"'s senior enlisted man, Sergeant Major Jeff Raker. Raker greeted Clem, a sergeant first class at the time, with the words, "Welcome home, but we're going to take a trip. You have enough time to repack your bags."

Raker had chosen Clem and four other men from the unit to go to Frankfurt for a meeting. He revealed nothing about the nature of the trip, but it was fairly easy to surmise it was related to the U.S. Embassy seizure. The men were taken to a secure facility, and CIA officers subjected them to an intense set of interviews and reviews of their backgrounds.

The five had been chosen to meet the Agency's simple criteria, which was to select two men who could enter Iran with foreign documentation and survive scrutiny by hostile security forces. There was no time to train a candidate; they had to be able to support a foreign persona now. Raker had 60 good men to choose from and in the end chose soldiers who could be quickly prepared for the mission.

When the interviews were over, Clem and John "Scotty" McEwan were selected; they would travel into Iran. The two could not be more different. Scotty was a wildly gregarious character who lived on the ragged edge of all that was prudent. Clem, on the other hand, had a serious, calculating personality. He had two years on the ground in Vietnam in a Ranger company, served as a Ranger instructor, and was a high-altitude mountain rescue team member. Where Clem sought out adrenaline, Scotty sought out fun. In military situations, that translated to wanting to have Clem at your "six" protecting your backside, while having Scotty out in front of you where you could see him. Now they would be dependent on each other in a very dangerous mission. They were given lightly backstopped identities and cover stories, with passports in new names. Before they left the facility, both were required to sign a secrecy agreement. Clem later said that:

> It was decided the first step would be to obtain valid visas from the Iranian Embassy, where a group of Iranian student protesters had occupied the lobby of their embassy and caused a lot of ruckus. Obviously the Iranians were very uncomfortable with their presence and me on purpose pretending to pay a lot of interest and attention to them. My plan worked, they spent little time checking on my docs, asked me a few questions and in no time I was back on my way to Frankfurt with my newly acquired visa.
>
> The second trip to Geneva, Switzerland, did not go as smoothly. After arriving at the Iranian Embassy at 0900 hrs and stating my business, they took my passport and paperwork and disappeared into the back. When they prepared to close for lunch at 1200 hrs without having called me I decided it was time for my evil twin Hermann to show up, I knocked forcefully on the glass partition and when a different official showed up, I demanded to know why they left me waiting for 3 hrs and acted very upset. Without as much as an apology his short response was: "Oh, we forgot you were here." He returned shortly with my passport properly stamped. I knew for a fact that they did not just forget about me, but had been checking my documents. The fact that my passport withstood their scrutiny gave me lots of confidence for my next planned trip.

The situation in Tehran had disrupted the United States's ability to collect information, and the seizure of the embassy by radicals presented a problem that was new and unexpected for the intelligence community. The military required precise information on the layout of the city, the U.S. Embassy compound, and the MFA. This was tactical information that the CIA did not normally collect. Additionally, the State Department did not maintain detailed construction data on American facilities abroad, so, in 1979, it did not exist. What was needed was classic targeting intelligence, all the information to plan a raid that would get the assault forces in and the hostages out safely. Moreover, the information was needed immediately.

In later years, this type of mission would be called an Advance Force Operation or AFO, but in 1979 it was simply an advance reconnaissance of the objective, and the team members were often referred to as "scouts." Among the questions that needed answering were, what did the target look like, who was defending it, what enemy forces could come to the defenders' aid, and of course, where were the hostages located? There were many more questions, and the military commanders needed them answered sooner rather than later. The State Department was able to supply only a few blueprints and plans of the embassy buildings and compound, while satellites could collect up-to-date, high-resolution imagery of the buildings and streets, but only a personal reconnaissance could show the ground truth.

Special Forces training produced the kind of soldier needed to do the job, and former major Richard "Dick" Meadows was another specifically chosen for the mission. Meadows was a highly decorated SF trooper and officer. Now retired, he was an "SoF" plank holder—one of the original cadre who formed the unit—who was still serving as an advisor to the unit. He would infiltrate Iran to meet "Special Forces" when and if the mission went forward. Meadows would lead "SoF" to the embassy compound, while Clem and Scotty would join Det "A" for the MFA takedown. Although Meadows had unparalleled combat experience, he was not trained in clandestine operations, and he was not prepared to take this mission on alone.

That said, he had the courage to volunteer to be the man for "SoF" inside Tehran. He would be assisted by Iranian-born U.S. Air Force sergeant Fred Arooji, who would act as his interpreter. But Arooji was also not trained in "clandestine tradecraft," and that was where the Detachment's operators came in. Both Clem and Scotty had the experience and, like most of the Detachment's operators, they were well suited for a job that went beyond collecting intelligence information; they had to be experts in special operations as well. There simply was no other unit in the U.S. military or the intelligence community with personnel who could conduct that kind of mission.

Meadows, Scotty, and Clem would also meet the assault force and get them to the targets. When the time came, the reception committee, codenamed "Esquire," with Meadows in charge, would meet the force outside Tehran and bring them into the city. But that part of the plan had not yet been developed. Much work had to be done to determine exactly how to get into Tehran, into the building, and back out again with the hostages.

As the planning progressed, "Special Forces," the Rangers, and the aviation component of the mission assembled and began to practice in the southwestern United States. The Detachment would conduct its training in Germany and join the main force later. There would be many changes to the assault force's configuration along the way, determined either by the intelligence received or, more importantly, the technical issues surrounding how the force would be inserted into the country.

When the mission changed from planning phase to execution phase, it was necessary to rename the operation. The original name, "RICE BOWL," had been deliberately chosen to imply an Asian target; the military wanted something more aggressive for the actual mission. The planners chose Operation EAGLE CLAW.

As Clem and Scotty prepared for their first trip into Iran, they pored over the available data on the two target sites, as well as everything they could find on the city itself. They studied street maps to pick routes to any of the possible evacuation points the assault force would be required to use, including the main airport, parks, and stadiums. Richard "Dick" Meadows had arrived in Frankfurt and began his work to put together a rudimentary cover. Luckily he had some good friends in the UK who helped backstop his legend. The men would travel into Tehran separately. They would stay in different hotels: Scotty at the Intercontinental, and

Clem at the Park. Journalists and businessmen favored the "Intercon," while the Park was hosting many of the new regime's elite.

It was early March 1980 before the team was given the go ahead to fly out. Scotty and Clem departed in mid-March from Frankfurt. Several days before their flight, they met one more time with a liaison officer from EUCOM, a USMC major, at a hotel near the airport. After reviewing the intelligence requirements, contact procedures, and emergency plans, the major told them there was one last bit of paperwork to be signed: a statement of understanding that the U.S. Government would deny their activities if they were arrested or captured.

Both men were incredulous at the prospect of being hung out to dry by their government, but it was Clem who now chose to be funny. As he handed the signed papers back to the liaison officer, Clem told the officer, "You know we signed with a disappearing ink pen the Agency gave us."

Clem later said, "You should have seen the look on the Jarhead's face."

Scotty and Clem had authentic foreign passports, just in alias names. It was decided that the first step before they traveled would be to get valid visas from the Iranian Embassy in different countries, rather than count on obtaining one on arrival in Tehran.

At the Pentagon, the overall operations plan came together. It was decided that the assault force would be transported by C-130 airplane to a refuel site known as Desert One, where the men would transfer to RH-53 helicopters flown in from the aircraft carrier USS *Nimitz*.

The airfield, chosen from aerial reconnaissance photos and debriefs of travelers, was surveyed by a USAF officer, Major John T. Carney, Jr., who flew into Iran on a de Havilland DHC-6 Twin Otter piloted by Jim Rhyne, one of the best pilots in the world, and Claude O. "Bud" McBroom, a former Special Forces officer turned pilot. Once they landed at the site, Carney successfully surveyed the unimproved landing strip and installed remotely operated landing lights and a strobe for the C-130 pilots who would turn on the lights as they approached the field. Carney did the job in less than one hour.

The plan envisioned that the assault force would continue alone by helicopter to a laager site [a military camp in the field] outside Tehran called Desert Two. There the reception committee, Meadows, Fred,

Clem, and Scotty—along with four Iranian-Americans recruited to be translators and drivers—would meet them and transport the assault force into the city and directly to their targets.

The Agency assigned one of its officers to arrange the logistics on the ground. Bob Plan had served with both the OSS and the CIA and following his retirement lived in Trieste, Italy. He was recalled to duty because he had the language and [REDACTED]. His task was to acquire trucks and a Mercedes sedan, make sure they were operable, and find a warehouse to hide them in. The Agency also managed to bring in a SATCOM radio that would be needed during the rescue phase of the mission itself. Bob succeeded, acquiring a warehouse on the southern edge of the city where he stored the vehicles and other equipment that would be needed by Meadows's reception committee.[1] The Mercedes would be crucial for the collection of necessary intelligence.

CHAPTER 4

First Advance Team Insert

Lemke's and McEwan's first trip into country was late March 1980. Once in-country, Clem and Scotty worked separately, coming together only occasionally at the Intercontinental in secluded, brief meetings to discuss what they had seen and what still needed to be covered. Along with details about Iranian security and the layout of the buildings and surrounding area, the two Berliners had to cover the primary and alternate routes from the warehouse to the targets and exfiltration points, as well as the route out to the location where they would meet the assault force.

Scotty covered the MFA in detail, surreptitiously taking pictures of the building, its entry points, and the security surrounding it. The team made 12 separate trips around the MFA and the embassy and, at one point, Scotty entered the building, ostensibly to get forms for the export of Iranian goods, and was able to get a look at the interior layout of the ground floor. He came away with photographs of himself inside the MFA with an Iranian official who gave him a guided tour of the building. At the same time, Clem was scouting the routes and collecting information on the security procedures at both sites. The planners wanted to know what defensive measures the forces would face during the initial assault and what backup the Iranians had available nearby. Clem also shot videos of the embassy, MFA, and surrounding areas—the combination of photos, videos, and maps reinforced the oral reports they would give back in Europe. It was the best intelligence the planners got.

While the men spent a lot of time walking the city, the Mercedes was used to run the routes. It was important to understand timing, traffic patterns, and where navigation might be difficult at night—all things not easily seen while walking.

The team departed separately from Iran one week after they arrived. Because of the tradecraft they employed, Scotty and Clem were very confident they had not been linked together by the security forces. Returning to Frankfurt, each man was debriefed in detail while photographs were developed and maps annotated. All the information would be disseminated to the planners and the assault forces.

CHAPTER 5

The Ground Force Prepares

It was not until General Vaught stood in front of the assembled JTF in an Egyptian aircraft hangar on April 23, 1980, and announced President Carter had given his "Go," that everyone positively knew the mission would happen, despite the plan's approval by the DoD, and having been presented to the National Command Authority. This fact was important for a dual-mission unit like Det "A." While a pure CT unit could focus exclusively on the Iran mission, the Detachment had continuous obligations that came with its UW mission. One of those obligations was to support USAREUR's exercises, one of which was already on the calendar and would not go away.

In the 1970s the Cold War was still on the minds of policy makers and the military. Massive exercises like REFORGER (Return of Forces to Germany) rehearsed the Allied plan to counter any Warsaw Pact aggression. In the special operations world, this contingency was practiced during FTX FLINTLOCK. Special operations forces from the U.S. and other nations would jump, swim, and walk into simulated targets in Europe. It was a huge undertaking from a planning and logistics standpoint and one in which the Detachment traditionally played a large role.

But none of the men cared about that requirement once the Iran mission was known. Here was a mission reminiscent of Son Tay—the attempted rescue of POWs from North Vietnam—and no one wanted to miss out. No one spoke of risk or danger even though it was clearly a risky and dangerous undertaking. If it hadn't been, no one would have clamored to go, just the opposite.

In the spring of 1980, one half of the unit's "A" teams were committed to FLINTLOCK[1] just when the commander and sergeant major needed to be able to look at every team member it had for possible deployment. Significantly, Teams One, Three, and Five were dedicated to the exercise that would take place in southern Germany in 1980 and, to avoid raising any suspicions, the sergeant major decided he would not make any changes to the roster.

The sole task other than FLINTLOCK that could pull members was the intelligence collection mission, for which Clem and Scotty were already committed. Members of the Foreign Ministry assault element would be selected from members of the remaining teams: Teams Two, Four, and Six.

This caused significant consternation among those who were tasked to support FLINTLOCK, especially as it became more and more apparent that EAGLE CLAW would actually happen. For once, no one wanted to participate in a four-week exercise and total immersion in Bavarian and Swabian culture. The dilemma was further exacerbated by the simple fact that the odd-number teams had some of most experienced personnel. Membership on Team One was almost wholly predicated on Vietnam service, and most of the team had not only been SF in Vietnam, but in MACV-SOG units like Command and Control North (CCN). Team Five was also one of the better teams and had coalesced into a younger version of Team One, with a highly effective team sergeant and team members. Team Three, the SCUBA team, also had many strong members who wanted in on the Iran mission. It finally came down to the fact that the Detachment's leadership knew the exercise was a sure thing, but they didn't know if the Iran contingency members would ever leave the city, never mind actually go to Iran.

With many factors up in the air, it became a difficult task to select a team for possible Iran deployment. Both Teams Two and Four had lost one man to the advance team, and Team Six was short due to recent rotations out of the unit. Early in the internal planning cycle it became apparent that the team which would be sent down range would be an ad hoc element put together from whomever was available. How would the team be selected?

Who would command the element was the easiest call, since Army leadership decided that Colonel Olchovik (or Colonel "O") would lead the Detachment "A" effort. Early on, it was decided that there would be no medics on the team, due to constraints on the number of personnel who could go forward and the presence of medical personnel within other ground elements. This further restricted potential membership in the Detachment's Iran effort by about six—the two medics from Teams Two, Four, and Six who were now effectively out of the running.

Probably one of the most important decisions on team composition was that of who would be the assault force senior NCO. The detachment had no shortage of strong leaders in this area, especially in the senior ranks. For Raker and Olchovik it was imperative that this NCO would be one who could efficiently mold this element into an effective team and train it to go forward. The criteria came down to a soldier with at least one, if not more, Southeast Asia tours under their belt and with special project experience as well. Team One's "Corky" Shelton was chosen as the assault force team sergeant.

For the rest of the team, different members were selected in diverse ways.[2] A two-week CQB course and a final shoot-off competition was held, with the top finishers being assured of potential Iran team slots. The only problem was that the top two finishers in this contest, Sergeants "Styk" and Jon, were both from Team Five. Because of Team Five's commitment to FLINTLOCK, they were out of the running. While they were excluded, the number three finisher from Team Six, Stu, an engineer, was chosen as one of the team who would leave Berlin for Iran.

The final group was diverse. Nine men would eventually make the mission, and they included one member from Team One, Sergeant First Class "Corky" Shelton the lead NCO, two members from Teams Four and Six, and three from Team Two. By specialty, most of the team members were weapons sergeants along with only two engineers. Of these, two had not served in Vietnam, but every member was a volunteer.

Although men had been selected, the mission timeline was extremely vague; no one knew when actual deployment might take place. This necessitated everything to be readied quickly. All the equipment was off-the-shelf from Det "A" or Berlin Brigade supplies, and the training schedule was, at best, fluid. The advantage the new element had was that all the skills needed for success were ones in which the element members were very proficient: moving, shooting, communicating, breaching, room clearing, rappelling, and driving were second nature to all of them.

In early March 1980, members of the element were assembled in the Detachment's second-floor conference room and informed of their selection. From that point onward the conference room would be the planning area for the Iran mission. Their mission was outlined: the successful liberation of the three embassy staffers from the Iranian Foreign Ministry and movement to a nearby park for pick up by helo and fly to the extraction airfield. The entire plan relied on surprise, speed, and violence of action. The three senior embassy staffers had been held at the Foreign Ministry on November 4, and had been kept there since. Their conditions of confinement were significantly different from those at the embassy, but they were prisoners nonetheless. The team members were also informed that they did not have to worry about how they would get into Iran or Tehran, or for that matter how they would get out of the country. Their focus should only be on cracking the Foreign Ministry nut.

The first decision that had to be made was how to actually get the three Americans out of the Foreign Ministry (which was conveniently located across the street from a police station) and then to the soccer stadium where they would link up with the hostages from the embassy. The entire group would then be picked up by helicopter and taken to Manzariyeh Airbase, which was to be seized by a Ranger company. The question of the hostages' location was solved very simply. U.S. Chargé d'Affaires Laingen was able to send letters and talk on the telephone, both with local diplomats in Tehran and with the State Department in Washington, D.C., since they had only been "detained" and not taken hostage.[3] He and his two comrades managed to send very accurate details about the room they were in as well as the security situation in the areas near them. After exploring options of storming the building by air and rappelling from the roof, the team's final plan was also the simplest.

The team would drive up to the Foreign Ministry, get out of the vehicle, walk up to and into the building, and take the hostages out.

The feeling at the time was that the element of surprise would give the team enough of an advantage to get to the hostages before their captors could react or have a significant advantage in firepower. If the team didn't achieve surprise, their estimation was that they would be compromised anyway. Early in the planning process a package arrived in Berlin from the U.S. that contained a detailed mock-up of the target area surrounding the Foreign Ministry.

But until Clem and Scotty were debriefed, there was a dearth of information on the physical layout of the MFA and the activity around it. To effectively plan its mission, the team needed to know how many people worked in the building, how many security officers were on site, and how they secured the facility. They also needed information on how many men were assigned to the police station across the street and how they were armed.

The lack of intel support could be attributed to two primary factors: distance and separation. Any classified information going to Berlin had to be telexed to the Berlin Headquarters or sent by courier. Throughout the planning phase most of the information came from Detachment leadership after each trip made to the U.S. or Patch Barracks in Stuttgart, the location of Special Operations Task Force Europe (SOTFE). In the days prior to digital secure communications, that meant long transmission times or a reluctance to send information through personnel who were not authorized to see it, even if they had the proper security clearances. The rescue mission planning was classified at the very highest level.

The second factor was that the Detachment was located far from the other participants. For operational security reasons, it was decided that the Detachment would not participate in any of the full rehearsals with the other units. The majority of the Detachment's team only met their teammates from other units when they arrived in Egypt, less than a week before launching into Iran.

These factors contributed to a large extent to the disjointed situation in which the team members found themselves. The intelligence information received from the advance team helped enormously, and the unit was able to prepare and train prior to arriving in Egypt, but they were largely unaware of the other units' plans. Although this isolation would not materially affect the unit's performance, it was a factor that would be highlighted in the Holloway Commission report after the failure of the mission.

Within this isolated environment the unit worked each day, and later and later into the night. First, the team had to formulate a way to get the three Americans out of the Foreign Ministry and to the stadium. Corky Shelton led this effort, while the commander and Sergeant Major Raker were devoting much of their time in Stuttgart and the U.S. working with other unit leaders and planners. By early April, the force received the first reports from the advance team and knew the ground situation a little better. Scotty and Clem had obtained good information on the MFA's layout, local security forces, and the surrounding area. It was enough to make a plan. About the same time, the CIA unexpectedly came up with a large amount of intelligence on the embassy compound that they attributed to a "Pakistani cook" who allegedly worked at the embassy and had recently left Iran.[4] While the Agency had little new information on the MFA, luckily the diplomats isolated there had been able to make telephone calls and send letters out, which pinpointed their location. That intelligence, as well as that collected by Scotty and Clem, was critical to the Detachment's final operational plan.

Around April 10, the teams participating in FLINTLOCK reluctantly departed Berlin, knowing something was about to go down and leaving behind the force preparing for an eventuality that was getting close. Despite last-minute pleas to the sergeant major, there were no changes to the roster. Those men not on the mission would hear about the mission's outcome along with the general public through news reports in southern Germany on the morning of April 25.

The team decided that the assault on the Foreign Ministry would be straightforward and direct. The team would approach in their vehicle and stop adjacent to a gate on the side of the Foreign Ministry nearest to where the hostages were held. Two men—one a fluent Arabic speaker— would approach the lightly guarded gate as if to ask directions and then neutralize the guards. Then, four men, led by Colonel "O," would follow and enter the building on foot. They would secure the hostages on the third floor. If necessary, breaching charges would be carried for use on secured entry points. Two men would stay with the vehicles as a security element to put fire onto the nearby police building and into any response force as necessary. This contingency was necessary because the Iranian Army Officers' Club was across the street from the MFA, and there was a building at the end of the street that housed elements of the National Police. Two threats, two men to counter them—no problem.

The entire plan relied on surprise, speed, and violence of action. Once the hostages were secured, the team would get out of the building and head off across town to the soccer stadium where they would link up with "SoF" and the embassy hostages for a helicopter exfiltration to the airport. The plan was simple and also contingent on the fact that they would not be met by a large force guarding the ministry. Nine men with small arms would not want to encounter a larger, better-equipped force. One of few pieces of good news the Berliners got before departing the city was that Iranian security forces at the MFA were few in number, inexperienced, and lightly armed. The team, by this time, also knew the exact location inside the MFA where the hostages were detained.

For everyone who was aware of the mission, waiting was the hardest part. At the end of each duty day after the team members planned, rehearsed, fine-tuned their tasks, and worked on their equipment, they would either return to their barracks rooms or to their residences not knowing when or even if the mission would go. Many leaders, from the National Command Authority (NCA) on down, were betting the mission would not happen. Many felt that President Carter would never approve the operation and that the plan was just a contingency in case the "students" started killing the hostages.

As April progressed, issues within Iran itself seemed to be coming to a head with more talk of trials or tribunals for the hostages coming from the revolutionary leadership. Each day in the Detachment the team would depart for the night and joke about how many minutes of sleep they would get that night.

Then, late in the second week of April 1980, Colonel Olchovik returned from Washington following a meeting with General Vaught, the JTF commander. He assembled what remained of the unit in the third-floor hallway for an announcement. He and Raker came up the stairs, stood in front of the group, and announced that the Iran team would be going forward to their jump-off point. The mission was a "Go"—at least in part. The element didn't know if they would be going to·Iran, but they were sure as hell leaving Berlin.

CJCS had only approved the final plan in early April. On April 12, the JTF commander was instructed to prepare for deployment forward. The planners determined the mission needed to take place before May as the increasing heat would affect helicopter performance. Additionally, the flight plan required eight hours of darkness. The nights were currently only nine hours and getting shorter. D-Day was set for April 24, and the execute order was issued on April 17, 1980, which triggered the move forward to Egypt.

On April 19, the Detachment's Iran team drove to the U.S. Air Force base at Tempelhof Airport. As the team moved though the city traffic in the Detachment's blue-and-white vans, each member went through mental checklists ensuring that he had each item needed. While most were sure that they had forgotten some essential item, in most cases they probably hadn't. The list was short: weapons, ammunition, more weapons and ammunition, and a blade.

Each member carried either a Walther MPK or an M-16 with as many loaded magazines as he could carry; at least one pistol, a suppressed High-Standard HDM .22-caliber pistol; as well as at least one knife. Both "SoF" and the Detachment also carried special "lock-eating" tools—devices that looked like a flare pistol and used a stream of burning thermite to cut through hardened steel locks and hinges in seconds—quite useful for opening recalcitrant doors. A final bit of insurance carried by each man was the equivalent of approximately U.S. $10,000 in Iranian cash for their escape and evasion should things go to hell.

The team didn't plan to carry rucksacks or a lot of food or water; they were prepared for one night's work in Tehran and little else. Their clothing was more or less "uniform"—civilian clothing under olive-green coveralls and a field jacket that had been dyed black and a U.S. flag sewn on the left sleeve. Arriving at Tempelhof, the team waited in the military lounge for their ride. It would be a C-130 aircraft that would take them all the way to Egypt; the same aircraft would accompany them to Iran. When the Hercules arrived, the crew got off and went into the

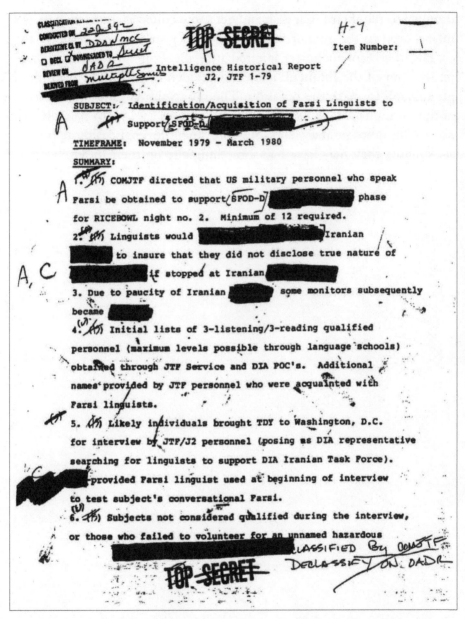

CLASSIFICATION
CONDUCTED ON 22 Jun 92
DERIVATIVE CL BY DDR N MCC
DECL DOWNGRADED TO Secret
REVIEW ON OADR
DERIVED FROM multiple Sources

~~TOP SECRET~~

H-7
Item Number: 1

Intelligence Historical Report
J2, JTF 1-79

SUBJECT: Identification/Acquisition of Farsi Linguists to
Support SFOD-D ▓▓▓▓▓▓▓▓

TIMEFRAME: November 1979 - March 1980

SUMMARY:

1. (TS) COMJTF directed that US military personnel who speak
Farsi be obtained to support SFOD-D ▓▓▓▓▓▓▓ phase
for RICEBOWL night no. 2. Minimum of 12 required.

2. (TS) Linguists would ▓▓▓▓▓▓▓▓ Iranian
▓▓▓▓ to insure that they did not disclose true nature of
▓▓▓▓▓▓ if stopped at Iranian ▓▓▓▓.

3. Due to paucity of Iranian ▓▓▓▓ some monitors subsequently
became ▓▓▓▓.

4. (U) Initial lists of 3-listening/3-reading qualified
personnel (maximum levels possible through language schools)
obtained through JTF Service and DIA POC's. Additional
names provided by JTF personnel who were acquainted with
Farsi linguists.

5. (TS) Likely individuals brought TDY to Washington, D.C.
for interview by JTF/J2 personnel (posing as DIA representative
searching for linguists to support DIA Iranian Task Force).
▓▓▓▓ provided Farsi linguist used at beginning of interview
to test subject's conversational Farsi.

6. (U) Subjects not considered qualified during the interview,
or those who failed to volunteer for an unnamed hazardous
▓▓▓▓▓▓▓▓▓▓

CLASSIFIED BY COMJTF
DECLASSIFY ON OADR

~~TOP SECRET~~

JTF-1/79 Requirement for Farsi speakers to be recruited for the mission. (Public domain) terminal to file their flight plan and get some coffee as the Detachment's men moved to the aircraft. Depositing their gear on the tailgate of the aircraft, the team members loitered near the front of the bird. Then, on the spur of the moment, someone decided to gather the team for a photograph to mark the occasion. The photo shows nine men in front of the camouflaged aircraft. They are of various ages, with haircuts that don't look quite military, and dressed in their coveralls. Although most are smiling, they may have had something else on their minds.

CHAPTER 6

The Advance Team's Second Insert

Between April 17 and 19, Clem and Scotty returned individually to Iran. Their job had changed from collecting intelligence and preparing for the mission to receiving the assault forces and moving them to the targets: the embassy compound and the MFA. The stakes were much higher, as they now had the responsibility for getting 100 men into the city without being detected.

Clem had to first obtain another visa to return to Tehran. This time he went to the Iranian Embassy in Geneva, Switzerland. Arriving at 0900 and presenting his paperwork, he proceeded to cool his heels for three hours. At noon, seeing the embassy was preparing to close for lunch, Clem decided it was time for "Hermann," his evil twin, to show up. He knocked on the glass of the visa office until a different official showed up, and demanded to know why he had been ignored for so long. The Iranian apologized and said that Clem had been forgotten and scurried off to get the documents. He returned in short order with a properly stamped passport. This time, Clem had the feeling the Iranians were thoroughly checking his background, but the fact that it withstood their scrutiny gave him confidence to travel. They were joined by Meadows during this, the execution phase of the mission. Meadows would stay at the Arya-Sheraton.[1]

Once back in Tehran, they had five days to recheck all the sites and travel the routes to make sure their plans would still work. Meadows got up to speed on the routes to the laager site (Desert Two) from town and the routes to the embassy compound as he would lead "SoF" to their target. Scotty and Clem force-fed Meadows as much information as he could absorb.

One small mistake nearly upset their plan.

Clem was driving the route toward the embassy with Scotty in the front seat. Dick Meadows was in the back, taking in the scenery. Scotty had previously walked, not driven, this particular "route reconnaissance" while Dick and Clem took a drive out to Desert Two and the warehouse. As they drove this route, Scotty was giving directions and told Clem to turn a corner. Clem suddenly realized he was in a bus and taxi lane, but the barriers prevented him from leaving it. The only breaks in the barriers were at intersections. Clem inched forward in traffic, hoping to reach the next intersection, but it was taking an interminable amount of time. As the minutes ticked by, Clem was not feeling very positive about the situation. Finally, the intersection came into view, but his relief was very short-lived, as several groups of Iranian policemen were standing on every corner of the intersection. A quick count of about twenty cops made them realize that this might not be their day. They briefly regained hope that they would escape their scrutiny, when a car in front of them, which was also in the wrong lane, was waved on by the closest cop.

That relief did not last long, as they were waved over to the curb. Clem rolled down his window and the cop demanded in broken English to see his driver's license and passport. Confidently, he reached behind the seat, searching for the familiar feel of his leather briefcase that contained all his documents. All he came up with was Dick's legs and, slightly irritated, Clem asked him to pass the case forward. While waiting for him to hand the case over, Clem looked into the mirror and noticed Dick's expression change from that of his usual confidence to one of worry. Dick spoke in a hushed voice so the cop would not be able to hear, whispering that he moved the briefcase to the trunk in order to have more room in the back seat.

Still unsure why that would be much of a problem, Clem told Dick that he would hop out and retrieve it from the trunk. In a barely audible voice, Meadows followed up with, "Be careful, there is some [unconcealed military] equipment in the trunk. The case is on top on the right side."

Clem now knew that he would have to play the role of his life during the next few minutes or Raker's prediction of him hanging from a lamppost in Tehran if caught would come true. Now he would find out for sure.

While getting out of the car, what Clem called his "evil twin" took over. He let the cop have it. Speaking mostly in German with a smattering of broken English, his voice got louder and louder to the point of almost shouting. Knowing that the officer had about nineteen other cops to back him up, Clem did not push too hard. The policeman reciprocated as he looked right in Clem's face with such disdain that Clem expected to be slugged any minute. His eyes did not leave Clem's face, and that was exactly what Clem needed him to do. With a fast hand movement that would have made Houdini proud, Clem opened the trunk partially, just enough to pull out the briefcase and prevent the police from casting a detailed look into the trunk. While this exchange took place, another more senior cop stepped up to the vehicle and told the first cop to step back on the sidewalk.

It seemed he felt embarrassed that the younger cop had raised so much commotion and felt the need to intercede. The veteran cop took the situation in hand, and, sensing the change in the situation, Clem immediately calmed down and became submissive to the new authority. The new policeman said that driving in this lane was a minor traffic offense and a traffic citation would be issued, which could be paid before departing Iran. They all apologized profusely. With the violation in hand and Scotty shouting out the lowered side window, "Khomeini is great!" with a raised fist for emphasis, they departed the area as quickly as possible.

While Meadows was mostly silent and breathing deep with relief, Clem continued to vent by chewing Scotty's ass for the unnecessary screw-up. Dick knew that his actions, although small and unintended, had almost caused the mission to end right there and then. He apologized in his own way, by stating that when they were stopped, he literally froze and was unable to think properly. He sheepishly admitted his only solution was to shoot his way out of the situation—unfortunately, there were no weapons available and far too many cops. Dick commended Clem on his training for such situations. Clem responded, "There's always more than one way to skin a cat."[2]

A day before the mission was to begin, Meadows and Fred had to solve a small problem at the warehouse. A work crew had dug a cable trench along the street that blocked the building's doors. Fred solved the problem by giving a bunch of kids oranges to fill it in so the trucks could get out. Meadows worried the ditch was a deliberate effort to block the warehouse, but then realized the ditch blocked more doors than just his.

The team was satisfied with their preparations and, on April 24, the four Iranian drivers were picked up and brought to the warehouse. Meadows and the drivers piled into the trucks and started out. The drivers knew the route only to the edge of the city where they would pick up Clem and Scotty. Thereafter, only the three Americans knew the entire route out of the city and their final destination for that night.

Scotty and Clem left their hotels about the same time and linked up, Clem picking Scotty up as he drove the Mercedes. They headed to the city's southern district and parked the car near where they were to meet the trucks, and waited. When Meadows and his convoy approached, Clem hopped in the cab of the second, and Scotty into the cab of the third truck for the drive to the rendezvous point (RV) where they were to wait for the arrival of the assault force. The three trucks headed southeast out of town for about an hour until they turned off the main road and went cross-country on a rough desert track.

Clem later remembered the driver of his truck smoked so much that he kept his head outside the window to avoid getting cancer from the fumes. The driver did have terminal cancer, which was the reason he volunteered to go on the mission in the first place. Clem was sure he would be next.

Finally, the trucks arrived near the RV location and were parked in a concealed fold of the hillside. The drivers remained with their vehicles, while Meadows, Scotty, and Clem climbed the hill with their equipment to the plateau above them. After what was nearly an hour-long trek, they crested the edge of the plateau and began to set up.

This was the laager site known as Desert Two. Once the assault force, the operators of "SoF" and the Detachment, arrived at Desert One by C-130 and transferred to the refueled helicopters from the USS *Nimitz*, they would fly to Desert Two and then move by truck into Tehran to their respective targets. The three Americans of the advance team would guide them first to the trucks and then into town.

Clem noted that:

> The plan called for all vehicles to travel together to a predetermined location on the edge of Tehran, at which point we were going to split up into separate forces. DF were heading towards the U.S. Embassy, while Det A would have gone to the Foreign Ministry. No one would have returned to the warehouse. As it turned out we returned all the vehicles to the warehouse before retreating to our hotels.

Meadows set up the SATCOM radio and tested it briefly before turning it off. He would turn it back on just before the C-130s launched from Egypt. He then told Clem and Scotty that it would be a while before the assault elements arrived. Clem said he would go to sleep and to wake him up when they were inbound. Meadows was a bit nonplussed, saying excitedly, "We're making history here, we're part of a big historical event." Clem still went to sleep.

The plateau was an ideal landing zone for the helicopters, and because it was slightly lower in the center, the helicopters could not be seen from below. From the top of the hill it was only a few minutes' flight into the city. The plateau was quiet, the night sky replete with a blanket of stars and the Milky Way twinkling above. To the south, the heavens were not as calm.

CHAPTER 7

From Egypt to Masirah

The Det "A" assault team arrived in Egypt in the early evening of April 21, landing at Wadi Kena, a former Russian airbase with its attendant bunkers and hangars. It reeked of burned and burning AVGAS. Colonel Beckwith greeted Colonel Olchovik and his team with a beer. The team members were shown to their assigned area and told to stow their gear and to get chow in the main hangar where the entire force was gathered. The main area was large and covered. As team members filed in, they saw well over a hundred other men from a variety of military services milling around. Each unit had set up shop in their own section of the hangar. Placed around the hangar were barrels filled with ice containing cold beverages. Each of the Berliners grabbed some food and something to drink, in some cases meeting old friends who had wound up in other special operations units. The unit members were brought up to speed on the mission; most of the participating units were in Egypt, and a few more entities would soon arrive. Everyone was waiting for the elusive "word" as to whether the mission would be a go or not. Even at this point in Egypt with most of the current special operations community in attendance, there was still healthy speculation about whether the President would give the final go-ahead. As everyone was in Egypt, it was felt that a decision would have to be made soon. The units could only be on the ground here for so long before the Russians spotted them from space and, during certain periods of the day, everyone had to be inside when the Russian satellite flew over. HUMINT (human intelligence) or SIGINT (signals intelligence) would probably reveal the American presence eventually as well. Further, with so many Special Forces assets absent from their home stations, it would not take an analyst or even a journalist long to figure out that there was something afoot. Despite all the precautions taken, each day spent on the ground in Egypt added to the mission's OPSEC (operational security) vulnerability.

As soon as they got settled, the Detachment's leadership went to work with other unit commanders to iron out the final details. Since the unit had not been involved in mission rehearsals and had only leadership-level involvement in planning, there was a lot to do.

While each element went over final details, the Berlin team conferred with their guardian angel, the AC-130H "Spectre" crew that would fly overhead to provide covering fire. The officers' club and the police building were discussed as potential threats, especially as the police were known to have at least two Cadillac Gage V-100 armored cars. The Spectre pilot said, "Not to worry"; he could hit "a bug in the butt" if need be. It was comforting to know the firepower would be above them.

On April 23, before the mission was given its final "Go," the assault force moved closer to Iran. Departing Wadi Kena by C-141, they flew to Masirah Island off the east coast of Oman. It was from here that the raiders would launch.

The final intelligence reports from the team on the ground were integrated into the plan while everyone impatiently awaited the "Go" order. Finally, two days before the actual launch, word came down, but not the word anyone wanted.

Corky Shelton brought the two engineers, Brad Cooper and Stu O'Neill, together and sat them down; both knew that it was not likely to be good news. Over the past days, the conversation had been about weight, specifically that there was too much for the aircraft. The Berliners had been told to worry about their portion of the mission and not to concern themselves with the larger mission; the larger mission was now going to intrude.

The basic plan was still the same: fixed-wing assets (C-130s) would depart Masirah carrying the ground elements and land at a site called Desert One. There they would marry up with rotary-wing assets from the Navy, RH-53Ds, one of the few active birds that could make the long-distance flight into Iran.[1] The birds would launch from the USS *Nimitz* in the Gulf. Because the helicopters couldn't refuel in flight, they would be required to land and take on fuel before proceeding on to Desert Two, where they would RON (remain overnight) and then move out the next night to Tehran to complete the mission.

Overall, confidence in the Navy helos and their Marine pilots was not very high. The helos had maintenance issues, and the pilots had not successfully completed a practice run of the mission profile. Simply put, the commanders weren't sure that the Navy birds would all still start after arriving at Desert Two or the next night for the exfiltration of the two assault teams out of Tehran to complete the mission. The lack of confidence led the senior leadership on the ground back at Wadi Kena to pare down the overall mission weight to accommodate a smaller number of helos that would be expected to make the whole two-day evolution. Everyone expected two to three of the helicopters to fail.[2]

This resulted in the Det "A" team being whittled down to seven persons going forward from Desert One, and the two engineers would not be among that number. Instead, they would be part of the ground team at the first landing site. The Berliners were divided up into two teams—those in the assault element and two in the ground team. The separation would happen after Desert One, when the two engineers would return with the C-130s to Egypt and the rest of the team would go forward to Desert Two.

The Detachment's job at the Foreign Ministry would be carried out differently than "SoF"'s at the embassy. Whereas "SoF" planned on going in full bore with an all-out assault to quickly take out the defenders, the Detachment's final plan, though daring, would be relatively low-key. A small VW van with the nine men (Scotty and Clem included) would stop on the street adjacent to the gate closest to the location where the three Americans were detained. Two men—one a fluent Arab speaker—were to exit the vehicle, one with a map in hand, and approach the guards on duty, as if to ask directions. Once at the gate, suppressed pistols would eliminate the guards. The team would enter the building and climb the stairwell to the third-floor room where the Chargé and his two escorts had been living and haul them back down to the street. Then the team would head off to the RV point to meet up with the "SoF" troopers for the helo exfiltration to the airport. Breaching tools would be carried to open any locked gates or doors met along the way. It was a simple plan that would rely on surprise, speed, and violence of action for its success.

Later that day, all the men were asked to gather in the main hangar for an announcement. When everyone saw General Vaught standing on a makeshift stage to address them, they knew they were going to Iran.

There was one final twist to the planning. Someone, probably a staff officer, decided that it would be a good idea to parachute two men into Desert One the night before the main force arrived to act as pathfinders and to provide intelligence on the local situation. It would be a High Altitude–Low Opening (HALO) free-fall drop, and naturally, Brad and Stu volunteered for the mission, despite the fact that neither was HALO qualified. "No matter," Stu thought, "a quick training session and a prayer and all would be good." Providentially, perhaps, a more senior officer got wind of the plan's existence and strangled it in the crib after only a few hours of life.

CHAPTER 8

Desert One to Abort

On April 23, all of the men assembled to hear a last brief by General Vaught and then moved to the aircraft. The hostages had been taken on November 4 and now the U.S. intended to get them back. The Det "A" team would again split up, the assault element would go on one of the first birds, while Stu and Brad would arrive at Desert One on one of the fuel birds.

When they heard that they would be spending the trip riding on a fuel bladder on an aircraft overloaded by about ten thousand pounds beyond its wartime max weight, they were less than thrilled. En route to Iran, all the aircraft stopped in Oman for fuel. While sitting on the runway in Oman, their aircraft was waiting to take-off when another nearly collided with it. Everyone laughed nervously and silently thanked God that they had averted a potential disaster even before they arrived in Tehran.

The scene at Desert One could only be described as hectic. The road team was on the first bird in and immediately deployed to provide security for the landing site. Then things began to unravel. First, a bus filled with Iranian travelers rolled onto the scene and was stopped by the road watch team under the command of "Special Forces" Captain Wade Ishimoto. A hulking Ranger stood guard over the terrified passengers.

Then a fuel truck blundered into the area. After firing a magazine of ammo which failed to stop the truck, Wade Ishimoto ordered a Ranger to stop it with a LAW (light anti-tank weapon) rocket. Its driver bailed out of the burning vehicle and made Olympic time to escape in a vehicle that had been following it.

As originally envisioned, the fixed-wing aircraft (the C-130s) were to be parked on both sides of the unpaved road, with the rotary-wing birds arrayed behind them to take on fuel.

On top of this, the Iranians on the bus watched all that unfolded as the fuel truck, still burning with flames reaching 60 feet in the air, fully illuminated the scene. It was a very dicey moment.

While Stu and Brad were with the road team, the MFA assault team waited behind their aircraft. They had unloaded the camouflage netting that would be used to conceal the helicopters at the laager site; personal gear came off last. As the helicopters were refueled, most of the pilots insisted that their passengers off-load.

There was a lot of waiting. There needed to be at least six operational helos to go forward, and what was thought to be the sixth operational rotary-wing asset wouldn't arrive until nearly 0300 local time. If all the helos left at that moment, they would arrive at the laager site in broad daylight. The feeling among many of those present was that at least one or two Iranians might notice six U.S. Navy RH-53s flying in formation over their country.

Through the early morning hours, the RH-53s were way behind schedule as they struggled through a haboob—a huge dust storm—and the loss of two of the birds. One sat down in the desert and was abandoned because of a mechanical failure, while another turned back to the aircraft carrier after becoming lost. At Desert One, the men were unaware they were already down to six birds, and the departure time for the night flight to the next stop had already passed.

Nevertheless, the operators gathered gear and awaited orders to load. When the final Navy bird set down, there were six operational helos ready to move forward, exactly the number needed for mission continuation. But that quickly fell apart when the pilot announced the last bird wasn't mission capable. Now there were only five helos, and six was the hard number needed to go forward. The leadership group on the ground, Air Force Colonel James Kyle, Army Colonels Beckwith and Olchovik, and Marine Lieutenant Colonel Ed Seiffert, came together to discuss the deteriorating situation. While the conclave was going on, the operators from "SoF" and the Detachment continued to load and check their gear. They would get another order once the meeting was concluded.

The situation was confused, and the scattered disposition of the aircraft compounded the problem. Men were in scattered pockets around the C-130s waiting as the helos that showed up were fueled and made ready for loading for the onward flight. Orders had to be literally run by couriers between the different knots of soldiers and aircrew. Soon after the arrival of the final helicopter, instruction was passed to load, but that order was given before the leadership group had decided the fate of the mission.

Then it came: the order filtered out to unload the helicopters and reload the C-130s. It was a surprise for most and simply a shock to many. The leaders had met, discussed the situation, and spoken to Washington and the President. The decision had been made in concert with the NCA: the mission would be scrubbed for at least that night.

For most on the ground, the reason for the postponement was not clear and everyone felt the air go out of their sails—the disappointment was palpable. The men moved their gear back to fixed-wing aircraft and boarded the birds which had been waiting to leave. One final hurdle had to be overcome: it was necessary to move the now non-critical rotary-wing craft so the C-130s could head back to Egypt, but at least they would be lighter now that the majority of the fuel they carried had been pumped into the tanks of the '53s.

This stage was relatively easy for the Detachment: they only had their weapons, ammo, and themselves to get onto the aircraft, whereas "SoF" had ladders and heavy breaching charges to load. As the helicopters began to move out of the way, most of the assault force operators were standing clear of the aircraft and watched the disaster unfold. An RH-53 was given the signal to lift off and shift position. As the engines increased power, the dust kicked up by the helo's rotor wash obscured all vision. Inside the aircraft, the pilot lost all his reference points. The helicopter slid out of its hover position and slowly drifted into a C-130 parked to its front.

A huge shower of sparks kicked up as the rotors tore into the airplane just behind the cockpit. For many, the first sign of trouble was the sound—a loud "whump" that reverberated through the area. Some would later say that it sounded like the area was taking mortar fire.

After the collision, chaos reigned for several minutes. Everyone had been complaining about standing outside in the cold night but now were thankful the pilot had made them get off the aircraft. Ironically, the only pilot who hadn't insisted was the one in the aircraft that was struck, but most of the men were able to exit the aircraft and calmly moved away from the danger. Many of the operators assisted the aircrew who had been injured off the two birds. One Det "A" and one "SoF" soldier would later receive Soldier's Medals for their bravery in entering the burning C-130 to pull injured crewmen out of the inferno.

The C-130s immediately began to taxi away from the flames, leaving some of the assault force to wonder if they were being left behind. Corky and Jim O'Callahan (OC) were standing together wondering what was going to happen next. Corky said something about being stuck in Iran and began to calculate how much ammunition they had if it came to a shootout. Corky looked at OC, and in his best bad imitation of Butch Cassidy, said, "Those MFs are in a lot of trouble." The tension evaporated.

By this time the commander decided that the area had to be cleared immediately. The C-130 set up to reload and, after a final check for missing personnel was made, started to move for takeoff. There was no attempt to destroy the helicopters left at the site, despite the fact that weapons, explosives, money, and documents were left on board. It was a fateful decision.

All the aircraft lifted off safely, but one of the C-130s carrying about half the Berliners hit a low sand wall as it was lifting off. Rumors swirled through the aircraft that they would have to ditch in the water, but thankfully it was able to continue and made the trip to Oman without further problem.

The wounded were discharged, and the aircraft again took off for Egypt once the aircrews had rested sufficiently. Whereas the aircraft were filled with the painful sounds of the wounded before, now the planes were shrouded in quiet. Just the constant drone of the four engines reminded them they were in the air. Air Force crew, Marines, and Army were intermingled on the flight back; no one spoke a word.

As the aircraft landed back at the base, the men filed quietly off the aircraft and into the main hangar. General Vaught met them and once again spoke to the assemblage of mentally and physically exhausted troopers. This time he had a much different message—he thanked them for their efforts but signaled the mission had failed. When Beckwith spoke he was overcome with emotion, and he vented his full frustration and anger on the troops. He would later apologize, but it signified the stress and forlorn hope the entire contingent was experiencing.

About the same time, two boxes were delivered from some British airmen who were present on the other side of the base. They had put two and two together and decided to send some cold beer over to the men with a note. It said simply: "To you all, from us all, for having the guts to try."

For the next day, the Berliners loitered around the base talking to their "SoF" comrades but still not saying much. They were really just waiting for a ride back to the city. The other units split off and flew back to Florida and Fort Bragg. The Marines went back to their bases. The Berliners had the shortest commute and would head back to Ramstein, Germany, in one flight leg with a C-141. There they waited for another airplane to take them home. After several hours, a C-130 landed and the pilot and crew got off to meet their passengers. The pilot was a one-star Air Force general and his co-pilot a full colonel, while the enlisted crewmen were all senior master sergeants. It seemed the squadron's entire senior leadership volunteered to fly the team home that night.

As the plane droned through the sky, Brad was on the ramp smoking a cigarette, sitting on a box. A crewman came back to make small talk and asked Brad what the brightly painted red box was for. Brad looked at him with a deadpan expression and calmly said, "Explosives." The crewman decided it was a bad idea for Brad to sit in that particular spot and smoke.

The flight back to the city was otherwise quiet and the men landed at Tempelhof in the middle of night, which was unusual as the airfield was normally closed. The Air Force had made an exception. The unit's XO, Major Robert Wise, was waiting for the team, and everyone loaded into the same vans that had brought them to the airfield just 10 days earlier. There was a cooler of beer, and everyone popped one open for the ride home. Back at the unit, they stowed weapons and inventoried equipment, figuring out just exactly what had been inadvertently left in the Iranian desert. The Iran team were greeted with questions from those who had stayed behind, but not too many and in hushed tones.

Two days later, the team met with Colonel Olchovik and were debriefed. They were given a week off and most spent the next several days in various states of inebriation, trying to get the smell of burning flesh out of their nostrils.

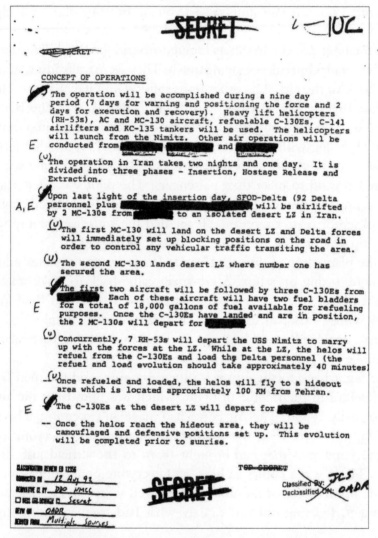

JTF-1/79 EAGLE CLAW Concept of Operation #1. (Public domain)

~~SECRET~~

~~TOP SECRET~~

C   (s) The Delta force will move by ████████████████████████████████.

-- (u) While at the warehouse, final preparations will be made for the hostage release phase.

A   (s) That night, Delta will move into Tehran ████████ and enter the compound early the next morning.

-- (u) The hostage release can be completed in less than one hour - most will be out in 30 minutes or less.

E   -- (s) Two AC-130s will fly from ████████ to the compound and provide on-call fire support if required.

E   -- (s) Concurrently, 2 MC-130s w/Rangers (61 personnel) from ████ will secure Manzariyeh. Two C-141s w/Rangers (14 personnel) from ████████ will land immediately thereafter and prepare for the arrival of the helos from Tehran.

E   -- (s) A third AC-130 from ████ will be available to provide on call fire support at Manzariyeh.

-- (u) Once Delta has entered the Embassy Compound and initiated the hostage release, the helos will be called in for extraction and transportation of the hostages and Delta to Manzariyeh.

-- (u) A separate fully coordinated, concurrently executed plan will be used to free Mr. Laingen + 2 from the Foreign Ministry.

E   (s) At Manzariyeh the former hostages and any wounded JTF personnel will be loaded on the C-141 which will be staffed with an emergency medical team. This aircraft will fly to the nearest US military hospital, ████████████ and then on to Germany.

E   -- (s) Other personnel (Delta, helo crews and 14 Rangers) will board the second C-141 and fly to ████████████ for further transportation to CONUS.

E   -- (s) The AC and MC-130s (with 61 Rangers) will return to ████ or to other airfields, as the situation requires. All MC/AC-130 flights from ████████ to Iran and return will require air refueling over ████████.

JTF-1/79 EAGLE CLAW Concept of Operation #2. (Public domain)

Tools of the trade: Walther MPK submachine gun and P-38 pistol, both 9mm Parabellum. (Courtesy of Doug Snow)

Team members of Det "A" conduct Close-Quarter Battle (CQB) training with Walther P-5 pistol at Rose Range in Berlin, circa 1978. (Author's photo)

Solo CQB live-fire room–clearing techniques at Rose Range 5 in Berlin, March 1980. (Author's photo)

Team members of Det "A" conduct basic marksmanship training with Walther P-38 pistol at Rose Range, circa 1978. (Author's photo)

Urban combat training in Berlin, 1979: Master Sergeant Russ Krajicek, Team Five. Krajicek is wearing the standard coveralls over "civvies," and is armed with the Walther MPK 9mm SMG. (Author's photo)

Ron Braughton dressed as Pan Am ground crew with suppressed Ingram MAC 10 at Tegel International Airport, 1979. (Courtesy of Ron Braughton)

Entrance to Detachment "A" Headquarters on Andrews Barracks in Berlin. (Courtesy of Doug Snow)

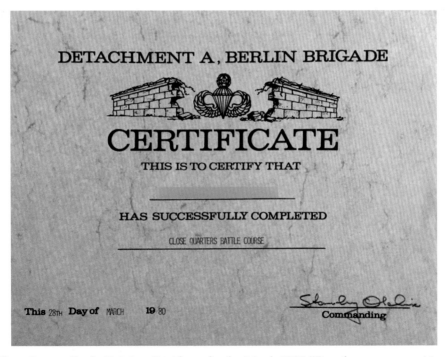

Close-Quarter Battle Training Certificate for the March 1980 "Best shooters competition." (Author's collection)

Team CQB training at Rose Range, March 1980. (Author's collection)

Det "A" MFA assault team preparing to depart Berlin for Wadi Kena on April 19, 1980. Left to right: John Mims, Billy Krieger, Col. Stan Olchovik, "Corky" Shelton, Jim O'Callahan, Stu O'Neill, Brad Cooper, Bob Kuenstle, "Sam." (Courtesy of Stu O'Neill)

Helicopter rappelling at Berlin Brigade's "Doughboy City" urban training area. (Author's collection)

Operator in "mufti" for urban ops with East German MPi KM. (Author's collection)

Jon Roberts running the GSG-9 "Factory" live-fire shooting house (mid-1979). (Author's photo)

CQB building-clearing training in Ruhleben, Berlin, 1979. (Author's photo)

Team 5 does familiarization training with one of Pan Am's B727s at Tegel Airport (Author's photo)

Helicopter training at Mott Lake on Fort Bragg. (Author's photo)

Night operations training in Berlin with newly issued AN/PVS-5 NVGs. (Author's collection)

Iranian Ministry of Foreign Affairs (MFA) in Tehran. (CCA image by Mahdi Shadkar)

Det "A" Composite Team at GSG-9 in 1978. Left to right: Ron Scheckler, Peter Kelly, Gentry Deck, Ron Braughton, Mike Mulieri, GSG-9 Guy, Henry Zelinsky. (Courtesy of Doug Snow)

Advance team photograph of Iranian checkpoint guard, March 1980. (Courtesy of John "Scotty" McEwan)

Nighttime counter-hijack exercise at Tegel Airport. (Author's collection)

Det "A" Composite Team receives GSG-9 wings from Ulbrich Wegener at the unit headquarters, St. Augustin/Hangelar, West Germany, in 1978. Shown are Peter Kelly, John Probart, Henry Zelinsky, Gentry Deck, Mike Mulieri, Ron Braughton, Jon Franson, Ron Sheckler, Doug Snow (off camera). (Courtesy of Doug Snow)

Nighttime familiarization training on board a Pan Am B727 at Tegel Airport, 1980. Left to right: Bob Hopkins, Paul Piusz, Max Reddy. (Author's photo)

Team Five training with GSG-9 in mid-1979. Left to right: Nick Brokhausen, Jon Roberts, Jim Stejskal, C.G. "Hawkeye" Thomas, Russ Krajicek, Howard Fedor. Kneeling: Paul Piusz, Chris Feudo. (Author's collection)

Iranian MFA model used for training. (ASOM collection CCN517402)

MFA model used for training. (ASOM collection CCN517402)

Team 1, Detachment "A" in relaxed training mode at Mott Lake, 1980. From left to right: Ken Norman, Clint, Corky Shelton, unknown, Gene Moyer, Nick Brokhausen, Jerry Merriman, Rick Hendrick. (Courtesy of Nick Brokhausen)

GSG-9 loved their Smith & Wessons. Jon Roberts practicing in the underground range at Sankt Augustin/Hangelar, 1979. (Author's photo)

"On rappel!" Vertical building-entry training with the M1911A1 pistol at "Fort Apache" at the Mott Lake Special Operations Training site (formerly "Blue Light") on Fort Bragg. (Courtesy of Lawrence Hill)

Advance team member Fred Arooji at undisclosed location. (Courtesy of Fred Arooji)

The "Mad German"'s hotel/taxi invoices in Tehran, April 1980. (Courtesy of MG)

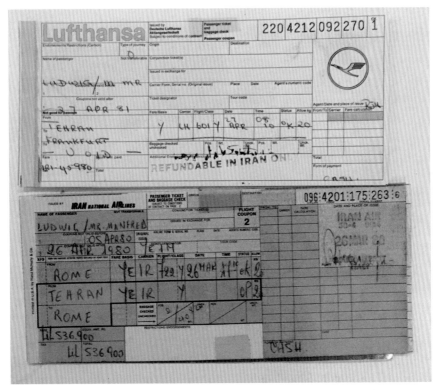

The "Mad German"'s tickets in and out of Tehran, April 1980. (Courtesy of MG)

CHAPTER 9

Desert Two and Escape

While the disaster unfolded at Desert One, the "Esquire" team was on top of their plateau waiting to receive the helos fully unaware of what happened at Desert One, two hundred and seventy miles away. They just knew the mission was way behind schedule.

Finally, a call came through on the radio, but reception was poor and all the men heard was that the mission was postponed, not that it had been called off. They packed up their gear, headed back to Tehran, and parked the trucks in the warehouse before splitting up and returning to their hotels for some welcome rest. They would be prepared to repeat the routine the following night. They were unaware that they were in danger. Now, they were really on their own.

The next morning, Clem was up and getting ready for the day ahead. He turned on his shortwave travel radio and was listening to *Deutsche Welle*, the German overseas news channel. Remembering the moment very clearly years later, he said, "I almost cut my throat shaving when I heard that President Carter had announced the failure of the rescue mission that morning. I knew we all were in serious trouble."

The broadcast was quickly translated into Farsi and transmitted over Iran's airwaves. All hell broke loose in Tehran. Thousands poured into the streets as the Great Satan's defeat was announced, in spite of the fact that no one had known Americans were anywhere near Iran before Carter's announcement. The situation was now potentially deadly for the team, as it would only be a matter of time before the local security forces put together a picture of what happened and, worse yet, recovered papers for the site that detailed the plan. That information included the location of the warehouse and radio call sign cards that showed a reception team was inside the country. Clem did not know the extent of the compromise but assumed the worst and realized they would have to get out of the country soon.

> We received the Abort MSG at the LZ. However it was so unclear and garbled that we at first assumed the Mission was only delayed and we were all prepared to do this again the next 24–48 hrs. We were not told about the Chaos and Crash at Desert One while at our forward LZ. Once back at my hotel while shaving and cleaning up, I turned on my shortwave radio to *Deutsche Welle* and heard Carter talk about last night's mission. Needless to say I almost cut my throat shaving while listening to that SOB. I then knew we were screwed and decided to make my way to the other hotel. Normally this would have been a 15-min taxi ride. But that morning there were no taxis to be had/seen because what seemed like a million people were flooding the streets and slowly marching towards the U.S. Embassy. Unfortunately my destination forced me to cut through the masses instead of marching with them. I did receive a few hostile looks and resorted a few times to raising my fists and shouting "Khomeini, Khomeini" with the best of them. I believe it took me almost two hours to reach the hotel. We got together and decided to get the hell out of Dodge the best way we could.

Clem got his gear together but left it in the room and went to find Meadows at the Arya-Sheraton. He emerged from his hotel to find the streets filling quickly with men shouting slogans, fists raised to the sky. He decided to walk and moved out along the crowded streets. At times, he would be caught up in the crowds and the subject of some very hostile stares until he too raised his fist and shouted along with them.

It was a tense two hours to walk the route, and he felt only slightly safer once he was inside the Sheraton. Scotty was already there, sitting with Meadows in a secluded part of the hotel. There were many journalists and other foreigners nervously listening to the crowds outside, who showed no special interest in the hotel. The Iranians had never interfered with them before and seemed to see this particular group of foreigners as harmless. It would be the Iranian revolutionary guards who would begin searching for the Americans when and if they put the clues together. For the moment, they were safe.

The team was dismayed. They had been abandoned without any clear notification of the mission cancellation or the President's announcement. Now they would have to make it out on their own. Staying calm and rational was key to success, and this was where their training played a big role. The team had several escape options, some worse than others—like an overland trek to the Turkish border—but only one quick way out. That was to leave the way they had come in, through the airport. Clem counseled against an immediate departure—rushing for the airport might bring more attention than waiting for a couple of days.

As the advance team prepared to get out of the country, a Pentagon staffer with no regard for security gave a "deep background" interview to a journalist the day after the mission was aborted. The briefing detailed the mission plan and the existence of the team in Tehran. *The Washington Post* and the English-language *Tehran Times* picked the story up and ran it, putting the team in an even more dangerous position.[1]

So they waited. They changed their flight reservations to depart three days later and waited some more. The drivers and Fred (Meadows' assistant) would make their own way out; as Iranian nationals, they had more options and needed to stay away from "foreigners."

Lemke, Meadows, and McEwan were locked into a course of action that could have ended badly at any moment.[2] On April 27, the three soldiers made their way individually to the airport. They had booked themselves separately onto one of the few remaining international connections out of Tehran, a Lufthansa flight that departed in the evening. Fred Arooji dropped Meadows at the airport and returned to his hotel to wait for things to calm down. Clem and Scotty made their way to the airport by taxi.

When Clem arrived, their aircraft was already on the tarmac. He could see the tail sticking up past the terminal, its yellow-and-blue logo promising sanctuary. But first they had to clear customs and immigrations procedures, and no one knew what to expect. As it happened, the procedure was easy—except for one small glitch. Customs searched Clem's briefcase and found several blocks of Iranian stamps with the Shah's picture that he had purchased as a souvenir. The officials wanted to know why Clem had the stamps depicting a very bad man they considered a criminal and "who deserved hanging." Clem told them he hoped the Shah would be hung as it would raise the stamps' value. That comment met with the officials' approval. He was waved on without any more questions.

Clem and Scotty made their way through the maze of stations and were sitting in the departure lounge when they glimpsed Meadows arrive behind them and step into the room. Suddenly, he was hauled back into the clearance hall by a man in uniform. Meadows had skipped an empty desk, but its occupant returned just in time to notice and pull him back. Naturally, Meadows had raised suspicions by skipping the desk and was thoroughly interrogated by the authorities, but his cover withstood questioning. In the meantime, Clem and Scotty died a thousand deaths waiting for Meadows to come back, not knowing why he had been singled out. They knew they weren't going anywhere, as five or six "students" with Kalashnikovs were stalking the departure lounge.

Once the discrepancy had been cleared up, Meadows was allowed to proceed and, after everyone's blood pressure returned to normal, the exit went like clockwork. The three boarded their flight and sat expectantly until the pilot made his pre-flight announcement and the plane pushed back from its parking position. Looking out the windows, the men imagined what might have happened if the mission had come off. They would have been departing on a USAF C-141 under very different circumstances.

As the plane's engines started, the whine of the jets only added to the anxiety, but it taxied to the end of the runway and immediately turned onto the departure runway and lifted off. They were out, but the three sat silently in their seats until the pilot announced they had crossed the Iranian frontier. Cognac was immediately broken out and together they toasted their freedom.

Fred Arooji, without many options, headed for his family home. There he met someone who had listened to the radio news and knew of the rescue attempt. Putting two and two together—he knew Fred had been in America—he asked Fred point blank if he was part of the American rescue plan. Fred, who had been drilled to "never break cover," made a decision and said that he was. Fred was told he would be helped because he had not lied. Fred made it out of country about ten days later.

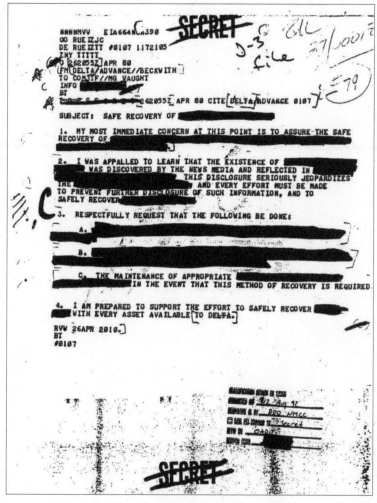

Message in which Beckwith expressed his concerns and frustration over the recovery of the remaining scout "Fred" in Iran, or whether the Pentagon has "concerns" about the recovery of the advance team in Tehran. (Public domain)

Days after Operation EAGLE CLAW was aborted, planning began anew for a second rescue attempt. President Carter, despite his disappointment with the failure of the first operation, was determined to get the hostages back. And while diplomacy was taking place, the military was gearing up for the next attempt.[3]

SECOND ACT

STORM CLOUD

JCS STORM CLOUD operations plan cover sheet. (Public domain)

CHAPTER 10

The New Plan

On April 26, 1980, the NCA directed JTF 1-79 Commander James Vaught to rebuild and prepare for a second rescue mission. The mission parameters would be somewhat different. For the next round Navy helicopters were out, as were Marine pilots. According to Meadows, during the five rehearsals for the first mission, only once did the Marine pilots execute the plan partially correct. The other times Dick was forced to break noise and light discipline in order to guide them in to the target LZ. In another event, Clem spoke with the USMC Command Pilot at the Pentagon to brief him on the best suitable HLZs (helicopter landing zones), possible obstacles, and other danger areas. After the brief, complete with pictures and locations of all wires in the immediate area that he and Scotty had taken, Clem said, "You're not going to let us hang, are you?" The Marine responded, "I promise you we will get you out, no matter what." He was the pilot of the first bird that turned back to the *Nimitz*.

For this round, Air Force transports and Army rotary-wing assets would be the ones to bring force to bear. The ground force would involve the same players, but plussed up to the point where the mission profile was no longer a "humanitarian" effort—it would be a rescue mission with attitude if it came off. It didn't, but there is value in looking at what was done because it points to the future of special operations.

The Detachment's target remained the same: the MFA. The Detachment's element was enlarged and carried more firepower, as did

"SoF" and the Ranger forces involved. Initially, the planners struggled with locating the hostages, as they were dispersed across Iran immediately after April 25. But as planning continued, the hostages were located in their dispersal sites around Iran by the intelligence community.[1]

The three Americans in the MFA—Laingen, Tomseth, and Howland—had not been moved so the Detachment could count on that certainty. Teams One, Three, and Five were selected for the mission this time—nothing else would interfere. There was some grumbling from Team Four, whose commander tried to argue that it was better prepared than Team Five. Team Five's leaders, Captain Chris Feudo and Master Sergeant Russell Krajicek, reviewed the record with the command group, citing recent training events with GSG-9, "Blue Light," Berlin's Sondereinsatzkommando, and the results of the CQB shoot-off in March, and the issue was quickly resolved—Team Five would go.

The approach this time was completely different than the previous plan. Whereas EAGLE CLAW relied on stealth and surprise, what was now called Operation HONEY BADGER would rely on violence.

★★★

Following EAGLE CLAW, the provisional intelligence collection team made up of Lemke, Meadows, McEwan, and Arooji was disbanded. In its place a new unit was conceived to provide necessary pre-mission intelligence to the assault force.

This new special intelligence unit was tasked to do several things:

- Provide covert/clandestine in-country intelligence for special operations forces.
- Develop and exploit targets in specific areas or countries.
- Prepare for, receive, and support any SOF introduced into a target area.

An initial recruitment drive brought in about thirty-five candidates for a grueling assessment and selection, first in Virginia, then in the desert of the American Southwest. The candidates were both men and women chosen not only for their military abilities, but also for more esoteric skills that would be useful in clandestine overseas operations.

The new unit would support the second rescue attempt, but, within weeks, the unit disappeared off the radar screen and has remained somewhere out there ever since.

CHAPTER 11

Berlin's Plan (Revised)

The Detachment's participation was codenamed Operation STORM CLOUD, a name which fit the plan well. It would be a helicopter assault on the MFA, with two teams providing security on the ground while one team stormed into the MFA to rescue the three Americans. Training resumed but at an intensity not seen in the Detachment before. Many thousands of rounds were fired on the ranges, while assault training and immediate action drills were practiced in as many different locations as possible. The so-called "Doughboy City" in Berlin's southern Lichterfelde-Süd district played host to a lot of nighttime training, as it was too close to the Wall and easily watched by East German guards during the day. An abandoned industrial facility in the center of Berlin was also used, causing a great deal of consternation to Berliners who tried to make sense of all the smoke and grenade simulators disturbing their daily routines.

While the building team relied on Walther MPKs, Remington 870Ps, and pistols for the inside work, the security teams went for M-16s and medium machine guns, in this case the Heckler & Koch HK-21. The HK-21 was a good weapon that could deliver a very damaging quantity of 7.62mm firepower quickly and accurately onto most any target. It had one minor flaw—it tended to jam when hot. The gunners compensated by carrying not only spare barrels, but a quart spray bottle of gun oil to relieve the problem. Each man's basic load of ammunition was impressive: the building team carried around twenty-five 30-round magazines per man, while the security teams were at thirty mags per man. Each machine-gunner carried over a thousand rounds of linked 7.62mm ammunition that included a mix of standard ball, armor-piercing incendiary, and tracer rounds. Two hundred rounds were carried at the ready, with the remainder on each gunner's back. Two M-72 LAWs, two Claymore mines, as well concussion and smoke grenades, completed the load. They were loaded for the proverbial bear.

A degree of irreverence permeated the training. All team members had olive drab T-shirts with the logo "The Empire Strikes Back" stenciled on them. An even larger stencil was made that would have been used to spray paint the same logo onto the MFA building in the middle of the assault. A 5-foot by 7-foot American flag borrowed from the Berlin Brigade Headquarters would have replaced the Iranian flag outside the MFA.

The unit was now out of the intelligence-collection business. There would be other activities undertaken by the ad hoc "new special intelligence unit" and other national assets to determine where the hostages were located as well as to conduct disruptive and diversionary attacks on the Iranian command and control infrastructure. If the mission did take place, it would not be limited to a "humanitarian" rescue; it would be punitive.

In October 1980, Colonel "O" told the force that they were going back to the States for further training and rehearsals. One last practice run was scheduled and, secretly, the force was assembled at a secure landing zone at Rose Range in the southwestern corner of Berlin. Just after dusk, three UH-1H "Hueys" flew into the LZ and the teams climbed on, Team Three in the lead bird, Team One in the second, and Team Five in the last. The flight lifted off and headed for Doughboy City. Flying a fairly direct course into the range facility, the birds did an assault landing on a road adjacent to one of the largest buildings. The security teams poured off the birds and set up in their blocking positions, while the building team raced to its objective. It was a full-on assault with few subtleties. Anything that came into view was considered hostile and "taken out." Team One ran up the stairwell, leaving a small security element at each level until it reached the third floor, gathered the hostages, and turned around, rolling up its security teams as it returned to the ground level and back into the street. Once the building team and their "precious cargo" were on board, the roadblock security teams ran to their respective helos and loaded. The birds took off, and then the assault was repeated. Colonel "O" and the Sergeant Major watched closely from different vantage points, making sure all went as desired before they called it a night. The helos flew back to Tempelhof while the teams conducted a "hot wash" to review and critique the practice. In West Berlin, it was the best preparation anyone could hope for before getting back to the States.

The time in Berlin was not all spent on the mission. Seeing the unit needed somewhere to burn off its excess adrenaline, the executive officer, Major Bob Wise, coached the unit's football team to the brigade championship. While the unit had mixed luck with its soccer team, especially at the hands of the Germans, its American football team was a different story. The brigade's teams were normally made up of young men in their early twenties, while the average age of the Det's team was closer to thirty, a bunch of (comparatively) old, grizzled men. One of the opposing players wailed, "What did they do, let those guys out of prison?"

That might have been one of the more positive interactions the unit had with people from the other units in the city. Between exercises, shooting, and city operations, 20 guys found time to practice and play. It paid off when the unit won the trophy early that fall and a raucous, if somewhat besotted, celebration followed to the tune of Queen and Freddie Mercury singing "We Are the Champions." Then, it was back to work.

CHAPTER 12

The Little Birds

In 1980, the OH-6A "Cayuse" helicopter had almost been eliminated from the Army's inventory. A venerable veteran of the Vietnam era, it had been withdrawn from active Army stocks and relegated to Army National Guard aviation units. Built by Hughes Helicopters, it was one of the smallest and safest aircraft in the Army and was nicknamed "Loach," for light observation helicopter, or "Little Bird." The military version of the Hughes 500, it looked much like an olive-drab, flying egg. Its fuselage was actually one of the safest designs ever achieved for an aircraft. In a crash, even though its tail and rotor blades would break off, its egg-like shape absorbed the shock of impact and protected the occupants. Still, the Detachment was taken back a bit when told that 12 Little Birds would ferry them into the objective area.

The Little Birds for this operation were provided to the 101st Aviation Group[1] from National Guard stocks in Pennsylvania, Oklahoma, and Kentucky and then assigned to the newly designated Task Force 158 (TF-158) as the Special Helicopter Operations Company.[2] Equipped with CH-47s, UH-60s, and OH-6s, TF-158—now renamed as TF-160—along with a number of USAF MH-53s, would provide the helicopters for Operation HONEY BADGER, the aviation component of the second rescue attempt.

Twelve OH-6 helicopters and two CH-47s participated in the initial training. The CH-47s provided command and control from the air, while the Little Birds would carry the assault force into the objective. To get the aircraft into range of Tehran, it was planned to airlift the helos by

C5A Galaxy into an airfield (the mission air head) within striking distance of Tehran, which was to be seized by a Ranger assault force. The helos would be off-loaded and put into flight mode within 30 minutes. For the OH-6 it was a simple procedure of refitting the rotor blades, which were partially disassembled and stowed along the tail of the aircraft.

Additionally, because of weight limits and the fact that the assault force had grown from nine troopers to nearly thirty, the co-pilot's controls were removed from the left side of the cockpit. Only one crewman would fly each bird. Instead, the front left seat would accommodate an assaulter, and two more assaulters would sit in the rear compartment. It was expected that at least three American hostages would be brought out on the return flight.[3]

The pilots were from the 101st Airborne Division and were all very experienced. Importantly, they were qualified to fly with night-vision goggles (NVGs)—an entirely new methodology for the time.

Training would involve the crews preparing the birds for flight in the requisite time frame, loading and unloading procedures, formation flying, live-fire exercises, and the assault landing itself. The longest night formation flight was approximately one hour, all done with minimal illumination and using NVGs. The pilots and the assaulters were equipped with AN/PVS-5 NVGs. Flying with NVGs was still very much in its infancy at the time, and the pilots were still perfecting their skills (as were the assaulters) as training progressed.

CHAPTER 13

Florida

While the unit's actions on the objective were being practiced in Berlin, planners in the Pentagon were working out the method of inserting the teams. The solution for "SoF" involved bigger helicopters, while the Detachment literally got the Little Birds.

The entire Berlin force was flown by C-141 to Hurlburt Field on the Florida panhandle for rehearsals. The MFA assault element was increased from 9 to 23 men. Colonel "O" would still command the ground element, while Sergeant Major Raker would fly in the command and control (C2) aircraft overhead. A number of the Detachment's support staff came back to assist in the training along with two extra men from each team—about fifty men in total. There the Detachment met the crews who would fly them in. They were from TF-158, a new, provisional outfit, equipped with OH-6 helicopters pulled from National Guard stocks.

The first briefings centered on how the birds would fly into and out of the targets, loading and unloading, as well as emergency procedures. Some birds would carry three assaulters, some only two. Daytime flights were made to allow the assaulters to determine the best load plan and where to locate their weapons. The tail security team wanted its machine guns to face the police station on infiltration to facilitate engaging any hostile threat that might come from that location, for example.

At one point during the night training, team members realized they needed a viable way to quickly recognize their team's helicopters as they sat on the ground. The answer turned out to be silver duct tape stripes on the rear section of the fuselage. In some contemporary pictures it's possible to discern the single or double stripes on each bird.[1]

Practice mission profiles were flown during daylight, and the pilots familiarized the assaulters with enough "stick time" to be dangerous, the theory being that if the pilot was wounded, the front-seat assaulter could help get the bird on the ground. Of course, there was no chance of that ever happening at night, in a hostile environment, with anything less than ten hours of practice. That said, most could keep the birds on the straight and level without too much difficulty. It was the transition to hover and landing that would kill everyone on board.

Then came night flying with all the birds in close formation. The pilots flew with NVGs, while the team members stared into the darkness as the birds went through their routes. Lit only by very small side markers, the OH-6s were all but invisible, and even in close formation, only the occasional main rotor blade of another bird would be sensed as it swished by just beyond the rotor tips of the observer's bird. It was a relief to end the flights, as crews and assaulters would be mentally drained after even a one-hour flight.

For the mission, the OH-6s would be loaded onto a C5A Galaxy with their rotors folded up in transport position and the whole package flown into an airfield that would be seized by the Rangers. The Little Birds were to be wheeled off the ramp and put back together quickly, loaded, and launched for the rescue. Simultaneously, "SoF" would be doing the same thing with its UH-60 Blackhawks in the far west. The assembly procedure was practiced multiple times until the crews and support personnel were able to make each aircraft flightworthy in several minutes. The assaulters always wanted to touch the "Jesus Bolt" that held the main rotor in place, just to make sure it was good and tight before the pilot cranked his bird up.

Gunnery practice was also big on the program, and ranges were acquired and set up for the helos to practice assault landings coupled with live-fire exercises. Anything dangerous is best undertaken in small practice steps before the full Monty is applied. That was the case in this instance as well. Static off-loads and firing came first, followed by single bird and section landings, before the entire flight was practiced. The pilots quite enjoyed the experience of landing 12 birds with 24 weapons firing live ammo out their port doors. Surprisingly, no one was shot out of the sky.

Only one mishap occurred when a wind gust caught the tail rotor of one of the birds and it spun out of formation.[2] Luckily, the bird spun up and away from the others and the pilot was able to recover and set the bird down in a field.

A final weapons practice was run at night, which was most impressive, as every weapon was loaded with tracers. The guns opened up as each section settled in to land and continued until all the birds were down. There was little attempt to conserve ammunition. The result was a horizontal wall of flame that reached from the birds to the ground and tore up everything in its path. The targets placed in the field were shredded by the machine guns, flopping over backwards as the bullets cut them in half. There were more than a few 40mm rounds pumped out of grenade launchers—using training practice rounds to avoid shrapnel damage to the birds. There was a short intermission to let the smoke drift off and to reload the aircraft. Then the routine was repeated as the birds lifted off to return to base.

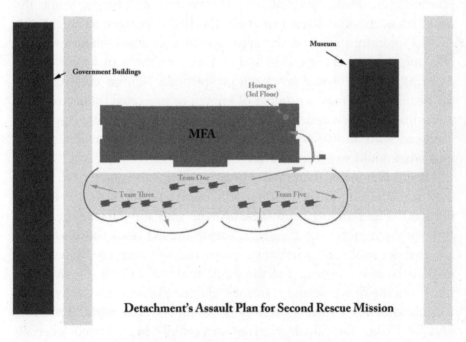

Detachment's Assault Plan for Second Rescue Mission

Assault plan of MFA. (Author's diagram)

The final practice runs were done at Camp Rudder on Eglin Air Force Base, the location of the Florida Phase of Army Ranger training. The headquarters building, a concrete-block, three-story barracks, was eerily similar to the Iranian MFA and would be the target of the assault. The landings were practiced again by section and then with the complete package until everyone was satisfied with the landings and placement. After that, the teams practiced off-loads and taking up their positions while the building team did its thing of retrieving the hostages and reloading the birds.

The daytime practices took the better part of several days until the force was ready for nighttime runs. Short flights preceded the longer ones until the full mission flight profile was practiced.

On the night of November 23/24, 1980, a full-scale exercise of the mission took place. The Det loaded its helicopters after a simulated unload and assembly of the OH-6s. The birds flew a nearly two-hour-long mission that simulated the extreme flight duration. Taking off from Hurlburt, the birds flew out over the swamps of Florida, while the assaulters sat back and tried to enjoy the flight. Further up in the sky, AC-130 gunships covered the approach to the target while a CH-47 helicopter provided command and control. For the actual mission, the AC-130 gunships would lay down pre-planned 105mm gunfire before the assault to eliminate a number of known or suspected Iranian military positions that included the Ministry of Defense. Having "Spooky" overhead with all its firepower was a comforting thought when flying into what could well be a hornet's nest.

The pilots signaled their final approach and sat down on the road, with the teams running to their designated security positions on the ends of the road. The building team breached the gate and entered the MFA, and within minutes the "hostages" were loaded onto the birds. The commander spoke the withdrawal codeword and everyone folded back to their birds by section, and the flight took off and ran for home. It went well the first time and it seemed like the plan might actually work.

Unbeknownst to the Detachment members, that night the entire SNOW BIRD force had practiced successfully in dispersed locations across the United States. The operations order for the rehearsal was codenamed "STORM CLOUD."

CHAPTER 14

It's All Over But The Shouting

By late 1980, the Iranian hostage drama had become a political football and it became clear the mission would not go forward. On Tuesday, November 4, 1980, the Republican challenger Ronald Reagan defeated incumbent Democratic president Jimmy Carter. Even before Reagan was sworn in, private signals were sent by the Iranian regime that the hostages would be released. With that Operation SNOW BIRD/STORM CLOUD was put into mothballs.[1] The Task Force broke up and the Detachment returned to Germany shortly before Christmas 1980. Everyone remained ready, but the release of the hostages on Inauguration Day on January 20, 1981, cancelled the need for any operation for good.[2]

Several days before the men flew back to Germany, General Vaught visited the unit, which was still at Hurlburt Field. He had made a whirlwind tour of all the different elements that were involved, and this was his last stop before heading back to Washington and the Pentagon. The helicopter crews were tinkering with their aircraft on the flight line, and the men from Berlin were sitting in the grass cleaning their weapons. Despite their disappointment over the mission being scrubbed, it was a glorious, sunny day.

Vaught was talking with Colonel Olchovik as he walked over. There was a bit of small talk with each man and then he spoke to the whole group to thank them for their work. He said "at least, it was good training." No one could fault his logic, but suicidal or crazy as it may sound, each man just wanted the mission to go.

TOP SECRET

DEPARTMENT OF THE ARMY
HEADQUARTERS, UNITED STATES ARMY, EUROPE, and SEVENTH ARMY
THE COMMANDER IN CHIEF
APO 09403

8 January 1981

AEACC

SUBJECT: Letter of Appreciation

Colonel Stanley Olchovik
Commander
Detachment A
APO New York 09742

1. It is a sincere pleasure to forward to you and the members of
Detachment A the complimentary remarks of Major General Vaught attached
at the inclosure. He has provided an unusual testimonial to the qualities
and capabilities which I know are reflected in everything you and the men
of Detachment A do daily as you remain mission ready.

2. Please pass my congratulations and appreciation to the soldiers he has
identified for their professional performance in this demanding training
exercise. The maturity, responsiveness, and professionalism reflected
by each of them characterize the entire unit as an outstanding organization,
one of which the Army is justly proud.

1 Incl
as

FREDERICK J. KROESEN
General, USA
Commander in Chief

THIS DOCUMENT IS REGRADED **UNCLASSIFIED**
WHEN CLASSIFIED INCLOSURES ARE REMOVED

TOP SECRET   DA81-01

CINCEUR General Kroesen forwards MG Vaught's classified Letter of Appreciation to Det "A" members of JTF 1-79. (Author's collection)

As the two officers walked away, James let the bolt of his HK-21 slam forward and said, "That's all she wrote then."

Staff Sergeant "JJ" Morrison summed it up best: "It would have been glorious."

The Detachment and its soldiers who participated received a JCS Letter of Commendation for their part in the mission. It was classified Top Secret and has not seen the light of day since it was filed away in the S-2's safe.

Timeline

Nov. 4, 1979	Embassy occupied.
o/a Nov. 7, 1979	Colonel Olchovik and SGM Raker travel back to CONUS.
Nov. 1979–Feb. 1980	Operation RICE BOWL planning begins.
Dec. 1979–Mar. 1980	Bob Plan acquires vehicles and warehouse.
March 24, 1980	Clearance for the advance team given.
March 25, 1980	Advance team members sign "USG will disavow you" papers.
March 17–28, 1980	Close-Quarter Battle course.
March 26, 1980	Advance recon makes its first trip into Tehran.
April 12, 1980	Teams One, Three, and Five travel to West Germany for FTX FLINTLOCK.
April 15–May 22, 1980	Asset control group FTX FLINTLOCK.
April 19, 1980	Detachment's nine-man assault force leaves Berlin.
April 22, 1980	Advance recon plus Meadows and Fred returns to Tehran.
April 23, 1980	Carter gives final "Go" for mission.
April 24/25, 1980	Operation EAGLE CLAW.
Circa April 28, 1980	Advance Team exfiltrates Tehran.
Mid-May 1980	Iranian drivers leave country.
June 1980	Fred exfiltrates Iran.
May 1980	Preparation for second mission begins.

Late April–Dec. 21, 1980	Operation SNOW BIRD/STORM CLOUD.
Jan. 8, 1981	JCS (General Vaught) Letter of Commendation to Unit.
Jan. 20, 1981	President Reagan assumes office.
Five minutes later	Hostages released.

SF Berlin—JTF 1-79 Roster

OPERATION EAGLE CLAW

ADVANCE RECON TEHRAN

Clemens "Mad German" Lemke

John "Scotty" McEwan†

MFA ASSAULT FORCE

Stanley Olchovik†	Commander
Jeffrey "Jeff" Raker†	Unit SGM/C3 Bird
Corky Shelton†	Team Sergeant
Stu O'Neill	Engineer
James O'Callahan†	Weapons
Brad Cooper	Engineer
William "Billy" Krieger†	Weapons
John Mims	Weapons
Robert Kuenstle	Weapons
"Sam" (Identity purposely concealed)	Weapons

OPERATION STORM CLOUD

HEADQUARTERS ELEMENT

Stan Olchovik†	Commander
Jeff Raker†	SGM and C3
John Pirone	Medic
Horst Duchow	S3 NCO
Jake Freidmanski†	S4 NCO Armorer

MFA ASSAULT FORCE

TEAM 1 (Recovery)

Joel Schenkleberger†	Team Sergeant
Rick Westbrook	Ops/Intel
Corky Shelton†	Commo
Rick Hendrick	Medic
Nick Brokhausen	Weapons
Tony Abernathy	Engineer
Don Lewis	Engineer
Ken Norman†	Engineer
John "Scotty" McEwan†	Weapons

TEAM 3 (Security)

Werner Krueger	Team Leader
Phillip Brown†	Operations Sergeant
Glen Watson†	Commo
Dave Boltz†	Engineer
John Mims	Weapons
Ronald Cornell†	Weapons
Howard "Howie" Fedor	Sr. Medic
Miguel "Z" Zamudio†	Medic

TEAM 5 (Security)

Chris Feudo	Team Leader
Russell Krajicek†	Team Sergeant

Robert Hopkins	Ops/Intel
Jonathan Roberts	Engineer
James Stejskal	Heavy Weapons
Thomas Merrill	Jr. Engineer
JJ Morrison†	Sr. Medic
Paul Piusz†	Medic
Dennis Patton†	Commo

†Indicates that the serviceman is now deceased.

The Weapons of SF Berlin

Two men huddled in the bush on the West Berlin side of the notorious "Anti-Fascist Protection Wall." They intently scanned the East German Border Guard tower opposite them, about fifty meters across the so-called "Death Strip." The strip was not mined—it was just a wide, open area of carefully manicured sand that was covered by the guards' machine guns, mostly the East German version of the Soviet AKM assault rifle, the MPi KM.

Under the tower, a wire mesh kennel housed several East German working dogs. The dogs provided early warning of any intrusion into the border area and were the objects of interest for the two men. One of the two men pulled an odd weapon out of his coat pocket—a heavy-duty slingshot. He loaded a smooth pebble into the sling and whispered, "Ready?" The other man put down his East German Zeiss Jena 10×50 binoculars, and pulled his own weapon out, a suppressed High-Standard HDM in .22 caliber. "Just in case the guards decide to get out of hand," he thought. He quickly ensured a round was chambered and replied, "Ready."

The slingshot sang and the pebble flew across the strip, into the kennel, hitting one of the Alsatians. It yelped and the others began to bark. Two guards tumbled out of the tower, looking for the source of the disturbance. But they were looking into East Germany, not toward West Berlin. The Wall was meant to prevent people from getting out of the German Democratic Republic, not getting into it.

An East German military truck came rumbling down the access road and stopped in front of the tower. Three more guards jumped out, and for a moment there was confusion as everyone tried to figure out what had happened.

The observers clicked off their stopwatch—five minutes had elapsed. It was a good test. The weapons went back inside their coats when it was clear they were no longer needed. They waited until it was calm before they slipped out of their hide, through the forest, and back into the city. In their civilian clothes, they looked no different than any other West Berliner, except they weren't. They were Americans.

They were armed and prepared for any eventuality, part of a clandestine U.S. Army Special Forces unit stationed in West Berlin beginning in 1956. The unit was sent to Berlin when the Commander of the U.S. Army in Europe realized having six Special Forces "A-Teams" deep inside Communist East Germany would be an ace-in-the hole should the Cold War turn hot. In reality, it was a "Hail Mary" plan—a means to quickly infiltrate over six teams of "Green Berets" directly into enemy territory to wreak havoc behind the lines. They would help to slow down a Soviet advance by sabotaging the all-important railway connections around Berlin, report intelligence on the enemy, and raise guerrilla forces to fight the Communists inside and outside Berlin. A formidable and—some would say—suicidal task for the men chosen to serve there.

Some eight hundred men served there from 1956 until 1990 when the unit closed down after the Iron Curtain and the Berlin Wall fell in 1989. On constant alert with a two-hour "string," the 90 men that made up the unit at any one time walked the streets of Berlin planning how they would survive if the balloon went up. Six 11-man teams, each with their own mission and target, speaking the language and capable of disguising themselves as a German worker or an East German soldier, carried whatever weapons or tools of the trade were needed for the task.

In 1956, when the first men arrived in Berlin from Bad Tölz where they had been members of the 10th Special Forces Group, they carried standard U.S. weapons: the M2 carbine, the M3 submachine gun, and the M1911A1 pistol. These were quickly replaced by the Walther P38 pistol and the Walther *Maschinenpistole Kurz* (MPK) submachine gun, both in 9mm Luger. The MPK came with a 10-inch-long suppressor that could be quickly attached in place of the barrel retaining nut. Both weapons were chosen for their caliber and because they were German. The P38 was in use on both sides of the Wall and was reliable within its limits. It had a single-stack eight-round magazine like the .45-caliber M1911A1, but not the same knock-down power. That said, 9mm ammunition would be more readily available during wartime. Dynamit Nobel 125-grain Full Metal Jacket (FMJ) ammunition was used with both weapons, not only because of the constraints of the Hague Convention, but to ensure proper feeding of the rounds during semi-automatic and automatic fire. A standard load was six magazines for each weapon; usually many more were carried.

The MPK could stand up to abuse and still operate even if it had been immersed in mud for several days (after the barrel was cleared, of course). The MPK fired from the open bolt, but it remained stable and accurate out to 50 meters firing single-shot or in short bursts, good for most urban combat situations. It was also easily concealed in the ubiquitous leather briefcase that each German used to carry his lunch to work.

But there were other requirements to consider, and other weapons were often needed. The "silenced" .22-caliber High-Standard HDM was one, and each team had several for those situations when rapid, quiet fire was required, like taking out a guard. Even more specialized was the Mark II Hand Firing Device, a single-shot, silenced pistol that looked very much like a tool out of a plumber's work bag. It was developed by the British Special Operations Executive (SOE) during World War II. Called the "Welrod," it was chambered to fire either the .32 ACP or 9mm Luger. Indications are that twenty-five thousand were ordered but not all were delivered. As many as fourteen thousand unmarked Welrods were dropped to resistance fighters in Europe before the end of the war.

Both weapons were used by Special Forces during Vietnam, but it was widely assumed the weapons went out of service in the late 1960s. They hadn't, and Special Forces Berlin had stocks of both; either the HDM or the 9mm Welrod were carried for assignments where it might be necessary to quietly dispatch enemy personnel.

Another was the Military Armaments Corporation "Stinger," a single-shot .22-caliber survival weapon that was issued in a metallic tube that could be disguised as a hair cream or toothpaste dispenser. It was accurate and lethal only if it was held directly against the target. When tested at the range, it was found the bullet would begin tumbling within feet of leaving the Stinger's short barrel.

Anticipating that it could be difficult to get to their assigned weapons at the unit's headquarters, euphemistically named "mission support sites" were established throughout the area of operations. These were caches, hidden containers that were buried and which held weapons and equipment necessary for sustained operations. The sites consisted of four "cache" containers that were sealed and buried underground in hidden locations. Each container was packed with untraceable weapons like the British 9mm Sten submachine gun and the Walther P38. Along with communications, demolitions, and medical gear, there was enough equipment for each team to carry out its mission and hopefully continue to equip itself through battlefield recovery.

During Vietnam, the unit, along with the rest of the U.S. Army in Europe, was severely strained by manpower requirements for the Southeast Asia conflict. Despite that, it had to maintain its war-fighting skills for the eventuality of a possible war with the Warsaw Pact. In the early 1970s, terrorism became a threat to U.S. forces in Europe. Student radicals who opposed the United States' involvement in Vietnam, as well as its presence in Germany, began to target American servicemen. The spectacular failure of the German hostage rescue at the 1972 Munich Olympics, as well as its success with the Lufthansa hijacking at Mogadishu, led the U.S. Commander in Europe to task Special Forces Berlin with yet another mission: counterterrorism or CT.

Using the equipment it had on hand and leveraging relationships with the Federal Bureau of Investigation, the British Special Air Service (SAS), and GSG-9, the new German Border Guard counterterrorism unit, SF Berlin organized and trained itself to take on the mission. The precepts were simple: study terrorist operations, anticipate threats, and learn how to defeat them. The unit's history with vulnerability assessments, VIP protection, urban combat, and intelligence operations served it well. By

1977, it was considered ready for CT operations—long before any other U.S. military unit.

The unit's Walther MPK submachine gun and P38 pistol were the primary "Close-Quarter Battle" weapons. But it quickly became evident that the P38 was not up to the task. After several thousand rounds were put through them, malfunctions increased, and frames began to crack. The 9mm Walther P5 was chosen to replace it—although many of the soldier-operators would have preferred the Browning P35 High Power because of its larger magazine capacity. Officially, the MPK and P5 were the standard weapons, but many found room in their load-out bags for their personal weapons. Colonel Stan Olchovik, the unit commander, and Sergeant Major Jeff Raker, the senior enlisted man, never batted an eye. Their unit was unconventional after all.

The ammunition load changed with the new mission. For practice, the teams often used Dynamit Nobel plastic training ammunition that fired a non-lethal, plastic bullet. The bullet marked targets but was limited in range and would not penetrate walls. That said, it was still dangerous and would wound if one was unlucky enough to be struck by an errant round.

Another round was adopted for operations: Geco, a Dynamit Nobel subsidiary, manufactured a 9mm, 96-grain round with a blue plastic tip that ensured good feeding in automatic weapons. After the round exited the barrel, the plastic tip fell away, turning the bullet into a hollow point. Again, because of the Hague Convention, these rounds were exclusively for CT operations.

Special Forces Berlin continued to operate in the city until after the Wall came down in 1990, and the weapons they used evolved with the times. Eventually the Heckler & Koch MP-5 submachine gun and the H&K P7 pistol were added to the arms room, but the remainder of the weapons stayed—operationally ready until the unit was disbanded in 1990.

APPENDIX 4

Training

Origins of Modern Close-Quarter Battle

"The end product of CQB training must be automatic and instantaneous killing."
— 22 SAS Instructor Notes

Close-Quarter Battle. CQB. Just hearing the words brings back memories of hours on the range and in the shooting house practicing everything from basic individual marksmanship to room and building entry dynamics with teams. Close-Quarter Battle is one of those monikers that gets tossed about like a salad. Everyone has their own version, which is a cautionary tale because not all versions work. But not so long ago, CQB started with a single and consistent methodology.

The principal pioneer in the field is, of course, William Ewart Fairbairn. A former Royal Marine and British colonial policeman in China, Fairbairn joined the Shanghai Municipal Police (SMP) in 1907. The SMP was manned by Japanese, British, American, Sikh, and Chinese volunteers. Fairbairn was both a street cop and a trainer—he observed both police and criminal tactics to develop better operational procedures. Later in his tenure with the SMP, Fairbairn created the Reserve Unit (RU), essentially the first Special Weapons and Tactics unit in the world. The RU officers were trained in what Fairbairn called "Gutter Fighting"—that is, how to take down the hardest criminals of the Triad gangs and their "Hatchet-men" when no backup was to be expected.

Fairbairn learned his "tactics, techniques, and procedures" the hard way—on the streets. After one nasty encounter and a lengthy medical recovery, he learned Judo from a Japanese instructor. After that, he picked up various Chinese systems. Incorporating all that was good in each, he developed his own fighting system called "Defendu." It was a complete system of armed and unarmed methodologies that he taught to the SMP and reportedly to the 4th Marines, the "China Marines," a 1,000-man regiment who served in Shanghai's International Settlement before World War II. Fairbairn's cohort and co-designer of the Fairbairn-Sykes fighting knife, Eric Anthony Sykes, the chief of the RU's sniper section, was at his side and co-developed many of their CQB techniques during their time together in China.

Fairbairn returned to England at the onset of World War II and was recruited, along with Sykes, to teach CQB to the operatives of the British Special Operations Executive (SOE), the forerunner of the American OSS, as well as commandos and the Secret Intelligence Service (SIS), also known as MI6. Additionally, he instructed the Home Guard's secret Auxiliary Units, who would act as stay-behind forces should Germany invade Britain.

Fairbairn was then detailed to SOE's Special Training School (STS) No. 103, a.k.a. "Camp X," located near Lake Ontario, Canada. There he trained Canadian and American operatives in his "quick and dirty fighting" skills, ranging from unarmed combat and knife fighting, to the use of small arms in close quarters. Probably the most important aspect of Fairbairn's methods was that he sought "to instill the mindset to kill an enemy in combat without hesitation."

Likewise, Sykes tried to do the same and ended all his demonstrations with the words, "and then, kick him in the testicles."

Key to Fairbairn's methodology was "instinctive fire." Instead of carefully aimed shots at fixed targets, trainees went into a crouched position and quickly squeezed off two rounds—a "double tap." Kill the enemy before he killed you. With submachine guns, he encouraged trigger control and the same double-tap method rather than full automatic bursts.

One of his training tools was what he called "the fun house," an innovative shooting facility his students preferred to call "the house of horrors." It was first used in Shanghai to train SMP office. and Sykes built a similar building at SOE's Lochailort, Scotlan base. It was based on a small cottage that incorporated pop-up targets. Trainees entered through the roof to engage targets in darkened rooms filled with smoke, disorienting lights, and soundtracks of gunfire and explosions. Fairbairn ensured similar training facilities were built at STS 103 and OSS training sites in the United States. These killing houses have since become standard training fare with special operations forces worldwide.

Another influential instructor was American Rex Applegate, who learned his basic marksmanship as a youngster in Idaho from professional hunter Gus Peret, his uncle. At the beginning of World War II, Applegate was developing armed and unarmed fighting courses for the Army when he was recruited for the Office of Strategic Services (OSS) by Brigadier General William Donovan specifically to instruct hand-to-hand combat, knife fighting, and pistol marksmanship. Applegate was sent to England to experience the training being given to British special operatives and commandos and the newly formed American Ranger formations. It was here he came into close contact with Fairbairn, from whom he absorbed close-quarter combat methods. Applegate came back to the OSS's Area B, which would become Camp David.

There were many other early practitioners of "quick kill" shooting, such as FBI Agent Jacob Aldolphus Bryce, a.k.a. "Jelly." He was a member of the FBI's "Gunslingers," a group of agents specifically tasked to engage heavily armed criminals to take them down fast. But Bryce did not pass on his skills. There are conflicting reports that he instructed at the FBI Academy, but the Academy itself has no record of this. Another SOE officer, lesser known today but just as formidable, was Colonel Leonard Hector Grant-Taylor, who instructed SOE operatives at a base in Egypt.

In the United States, with the dissolution of the OSS and the Rangers after World War II, much of the expertise associated with CQB was lost or subordinated to other, less complicated (and easier to teach) marksmanship training. On the whole, the Korean and Vietnam conflicts did not require the same close-quarters fighting skills, although the Marines and Army kept up "quick-kill" rifle training to some degree. In 1990, the USMC even reissued *Shooting to Live*, a book written by Fairbairn and Sykes in 1942, as a reference publication called FMFRP-12-81, an indication of the considered value of their skills. The instruction and techniques which Fairbairn, Sykes, and Applegate developed serve as the foundation for modern CQB.

Jeff Cooper is probably the best known of combat shooting "influencers." In the 1960s and 1970s, Cooper emerged as the American father of the "modern technique" of shooting. Cooper, a U.S. Marine, developed a style that included the "Weaver Stance," a two-handed pistol grip used in competition that differed slightly from Fairbairn's stance. Cooper adapted his from that used by California County Deputy Jack Weaver for shooting competitions. It featured isometric tension through a "push-pull" holding technique. Cooper's techniques have been woven into practical pistol instruction and adopted by many police units.

It was the 1970s when CQB began to make its resurgence in the U.S. military. But it had already done so in the United Kingdom, spurred by the 22nd Special Air Service Regiment's operations in Aden during the mid-1960s. Fighting an insurgency in urban areas highlighted the need for tactics to eliminate a hostile terrorist threat that might emerge in the middle of an unarmed civilian crowd. That required being able to eliminate the threat completely without endangering innocent lives. In 1966, the 22nd SAS Regiment started a CQB course to fill that need. Its basic requirement was for an undercover operator (in civilian clothing) to draw his weapon and fire six rounds into a playing card at 15 meters. This was followed by the creation of the Counter Revolutionary Warfare (CRW) Wing, a specialist group of trainers initially created as a response to rising terrorism in Europe and especially the 1972 Munich Olympic massacre in Germany. The CRW was (and remains) responsible for training the entire cadre of operational SAS soldiers in CQB counterterrorist (CT) tactics, as well as selected troopers for bodyguard (BG) operations. Once trained, the SAS squadrons would rotate to serve in what was first called "Pagoda Troop" and later the "Special Project Teams" on standby for CT incidents. Its first acknowledged mission was the successful 1980 assault of the Iranian Embassy at Prince's Gate in London, which ended with 19 hostages rescued and five of six terrorists killed in an 11-minute takedown dubbed "Operation NIMROD."

In the early 1970s, the rise of terrorism in Europe had begun to make U.S. Government leadership uneasy. Slowly, efforts were launched to form counterterrorism-capable units to combat it. Quickly ruling out military police units as inappropriate, the task fell to the U.S. Army Special Forces. In Europe—the epicenter of terrorist incidents against American interests—Special Forces Berlin was tasked to form an "anti-hijacking" capability by the U.S. European Command in 1975. Close-Quarter Battle would form the core of its initial train-up. Instruction was developed and presented by the unit's soldiers who had served with MACV-SOG along with several who had served with the 22nd SAS and been trained in CQB and BG tactics. SF Berlin would be followed by other units trained for the CT mission, including the short-lived 5th SF Group's "Blue Light" program and others. Many other nations launched similar programs during that period, Israel, Germany, and France among them.

No matter the origin, it is important to note that CQB techniques have never been fixed in their presentation but are always adaptable to the situation and the weapons used. The key to CQB therefore is not the instruments used but the spirit behind them.

Special Air Services Close-Quarter Battle (CQB) Mindset

Introduction

The aim of CQB training is to guarantee success in killing. It is much more of a personal affair than ordinary combat and it is just not good enough to temporarily put your opponent out of action so that he can live to fight another day, He must be definitively and quickly killed, so that you can switch your whole attention onto the next target.

Besides obvious physical abilities, the CQB operator must be cool-headed and above all, remorseless.

Opponents must never be given "gentlemanly" chances. He must be kicked whilst he is down, so that he stays down. This is imperative.

The pistol and submachine gun are the main weapons used by the CQB operator. These weapons are generally regarded by the ignorant as "dangerous" and "useless". In the hands of a trained CQB operator, these weapons are extremely lethal. However, for the CQB operator to maintain a high degree of professionalism he must train continuously in an aggressive manner.

The end product of CQB training must be automatic and instantaneous killing.

The general coverage of CQB falls under six headings:

a. Surprise—The operator must gain complete surprise over his opponents in all possible situations. This is achieved by good intelligence, planning, briefing, method of approach, choice of weapon for the job, choice of footwear, etc. If these principles are adhered to, they will result in the success the operation, and also ensure that the operator himself is never surprised.

b. Confidence—Successful CQB is largely a matter of confidence. Confidence in himself, the situation, and his weapon play a very big part in ensuring the success of an operator. The confident handling of his weapon makes lethal CQB shooting from almost any angle as easy as punching a drunk on the nose.

c. Concentration—Another abbreviation of close-quarter battles could well be CTK (Concentrate to Kill). The operator shoots to kill, not hit. He must build up a clear, defined picture of every aspect of the job in hand. Nothing must distract him from his purpose of killing in a systematic fashion.

The mind does wander quite easily, but this must not be tolerated in CQB. It must be emphatically stressed upon from the moment the student starts his training. A wandering mind is usually detected in training by a fall-off in results and, of course, in the real thing by a vacancy for a new operator arising.

d. Speed—In CQB, contact is over in a matter of split seconds. Therefore speed is vital but it must be the correct type of speed. The mad, wild, plan-less rush is not only foolish, but in most cases, catastrophical [sic]. The speed must be of a cool, unruffled deliberate nature. Accuracy and success go naturally with this speed. The tempo of all CQB is "Careful Hurry". This tempo must be adhered to throughout the training. Keenness and excitement are natural amongst students, but it does develop the incorrect sort of speed. It must be stamped out from the word "Go". The Battle-crouch with its ensuing good, deft footwork, must be strictly adopted. An excited student will get himself into the oddest firing positions and so become off balance. The CQB Operator must never become flustered and stray from the "Careful Hurry".

e. Teamwork—Individual CQB operators in Special Forces are exceptional and normal operations are carried out by small teams or patrols. Due to the close proximity and speed of the participants in CQB, the absolute essence of teamwork is of primary importance. Who goes where and when. Who kills whom and how. Synchronized timing, etc. must be spot on. A team going on an operation must be given all the time possible to study their target and plan its execution. They must rehearse time and time again, taking into account all the possibilities of target routine change. After initial CQB training, students should be made to work in pairs, covering each other during tactical approach and withdrawal etc. Afterwards add a third and fourth man building up to patrol strength.

f. Offensive Attitude—In CQB from the very start, the gloves are off. It is a simple matter of "his life, or yours". Squeamishness, pity, remorse or mistakes are fatal. Nothing should be done in self-defense. All actions must be of an extremely offensive nature. Operators should develop a hatred and contempt for the opposition, but, never, never, underestimate him.

Students should be edged into this determined and offensive spirit from the commencement of training.

— Extracted from a UK 22SASR training document.

Close-Quarter Battle Training Plan Outline (Two Weeks)

The Detachment "A" Close-Quarter Battle course was one of several that aimed to ensure tactics were uniform throughout the unit. That was not to say tactics were set in stone—there was a starting point (at a very advanced level) accomplished by training that would be modified as experience showed better methods. What is illustrated here is an example of a two-week period of instruction that was given to all team members.

All training began with familiarization and marksmanship with assigned weapons. (Walther MPK submachine gun, Walther P-1 pistol, which was soon replaced by the Walther P-5 pistol.) Additionally, special weapons such as the silenced Welrod and the suppressed High-Standard HDM were brought into training only after the other weapons were mastered.

Initial training commenced with basic familiarization including disassembly, assembly, loading, unloading, standard functioning, and handling misfires before loaded weapons were introduced.

Actual live marksmanship began with slow aimed fire using off-hand and Weaver stances. Once the shooter had mastered hitting a bullseye at 7, 10, and 20 meters, they would progress into instinctive or quick-fire training, with the desired end result being consistent and consecutive hits within the target's kill zone.

The training was designed to escalate in intensity through constant drill which tested spatial awareness—especially important in room-clearing exercises—and focus on details that determined possible threats. Key attributes of training were repetition and speed, which gave the shooter total familiarity with his weapons and muscle memory for all his actions.

What follows is a typical two-week course of instruction:

Basic Single Target Drill

NRA (National Rifle Association) bullseye—slow aimed, double-tap, and rapid fire. 7m, 10m, 20m

Silhouette—double-tap and rapid fire. 7m, 10m, 20m

Turn and fire drills—90° and 180° rotation in place
Firing from behind cover—walls, door frames
Target discrimination drills
- By numbers (using chalked targets), by colors (using balloons)

Shoot/don't shoot judgment drills
- Bad guy/good guy targets

Multiple Target Drills

Called shots by numbers (chalked targets), by colors (balloons)
Bad guy/good guy (image targets)
Weapon reloads (standard and short loads), stoppages w/ dummy rounds in magazines

Weapon transition
- From SMG to pistol
- From pistol to SMG

Movement
- Solo operator
- Two-man team
- Assault team

Shooting on the move

Room clearing drills

Building searches (individual and team)

Shooting from and around vehicles

Low visibility operations (undercover, VIP close protection drills)

STANDARDS
- Load, unload, and reload
- Slow and rapid fire to score
- Group consistently without major error (miss hostile, kill friendly)

- Correct basic stoppages, reload safely, and on time
- Move safely alone and by team
- Maintain safety, trigger finger awareness, and muzzle awareness at all times
- Perform weapons maintenance and function checks

SF Berlin Weapons Inventory

1957–63

    M3 .45-caliber submachine gun
    M2 .30-caliber carbine
    M1911A1 .45-caliber pistol
    Welrod 9mm silenced pistol★
    Sten 9mm submachine gun★
    Walther P38 9mm pistol
    High Standard HDM(S) .22-caliber suppressed pistol★

1963–84

    Walther MPK w/ silencer
    Walther P38 9mm pistol
    Stinger .22-caliber one-shot concealment weapon★
    MPi KM & MPi KMmS (East German AK-47) 7.62×39mm assault
       rifle★
    Ingram MAC 10/11 submachine gun
    M79 40mm grenade launcher★
    M60 machine gun★
    M79 Pyronal Thermal Torch★
    Walther P5 9mm pistol
    H&K 21A1 7.62mm machine gun★
    40-XB 7.62mm sniper rifle w/ Leupold Telescopic sight★
    XM21 System 7.62mm with Redfield ART 3–9×Telescopic sight★
    Remington 870P 12-gauge shotgun★

1984–90

    MP5 9mm submachine gun
    MP5SD 9mm suppressed submachine gun
    MP5K 9mm submachine gun
    H&K P7 9mm pistol
    Beretta M9 9mm pistol
    H&K PSG1 7.62mm sniper rifle w/ Hensoldt 6×42 Telescopic sight
    McMillan Tactical 700 .300WM rifle w/ Leupold 6.5–20 Mark 4
       Telescopic sight

★Also in the inventory until 1990.

Interviews

Colonel Stanley Olchovik, Commander, Detachment "A"

A native of Czechoslovakia, Stan Olchovik escaped his home country at the onset of World War II and fled to France. Details are murky, but it is said that he joined the French Resistance to fight their Nazi oppressors and, after the war, immigrated to the United States.

Joining the U.S. Army as an artillery officer in 1950, he served in Vietnam and then joined Special Forces. He was assigned to command Detachment "A" in 1976 and stayed with the unit until 1981. He retired in 1985 after 35 years of service; the last position he held was of Commander, Joint Unconventional Warfare Task Force, Atlantic.

Olchovik was well respected by the men of Det "A" and feared by the Russians in East Germany. The commander of Soviet Forces once asked Colonel Olchovik if "your men are going to kidnap me tonight," while both were attending a gala event in Potsdam, GDR. He wasn't kidnapped, but other things happened (a story for another time).

In 1993, Colonel "O" as he was known to the men, helped convince a would-be Azerbaijani hijacker of a Russian AEROFLOT airliner to give himself up to the police. Olchovik, who spoke Azerbaijani Russian as well as German, French, and his native Czech, persuaded the man to put the pin back in the grenade he brandished.

This interview first appeared in: "Desert One and Operation Eagle Claw," interview with Col Stanley Olchovik, Special Forces: The First Fifty Years,

Tampa: Faircount LLC for the Special Forces Association, 2002. On April 3, 2001, Dr. Kenn Finlayson, USAJFKSWCS Command Historian, interviewed Olchovik.

Q: What was the background on your participation in Operation EAGLE CLAW?

A: When the authorities made the decision to study the liberation of our people in Iran, they started looking for intelligence sources. Little was available, because whatever the Shah of Iran installed there—and when I was in the 10th Group I was involved with it—it was all destroyed. So they started looking for people who were readily available to go there with a good cover, good documentation and a good story. We were told that the Agency [CIA] "will interview five of your people and select those that will go initially to Iran." So I picked up five people; Lemke and McEwan were among them. And they went up there and they interviewed, and they said, "Well, we really don't need five people at this time, so we'll select two." I said, "Okay, let me know." And they did. So Lemke and McEwan went up there the first trip. And that was around, I believe, in March 1980.

Finally, a decision was made, at that time, but Charlie [Beckwith] never stated that they said okay. He said, "I cannot handle the ministry (ministry of Defense, where three hostages were being held), so find somebody who could handle the ministry." And that's when I said, "Okay, hell, I can handle the ministry." So my guys went up there and scouted the ministry as well as the embassy. They came back, came here and briefed Charlie and told him there was a nice ground, a nice landing place right across the street for the helicopter. So he said, "Well, make your plans."

And so plans were made, they were rehearsed, rehearsed, rehearsed, rehearsed. We came here and rehearsed with Charlie and went back and waited for orders to deploy. And we went ahead through a lengthy process, and our job was to stay in communication with "SoF," the AC-130s and the helicopters, the Stallions. So I carried three radios with me. And, you know, all kinds of call signs and all kinds of stuff for the possible areas around my particular place around the ministry; pick out the good areas to strike. We wrote extensive plans; I still have them handwritten, for attacking this particular target.

Weapons were no problem.

Q: What was your experience when you landed at the Desert One Site?
A: When we landed, the first thing that surprised me was a burning oil truck... the whole sky was lit up. The Rangers had flown in before us, and they thought (well some private) thought that it was a threat! That goddamn thing was blazing all over the place! Finally we got the word that COL Pittman, from the radio, learned of the distress call of a helicopter that landed in the desert, and went to rescue them. He was the one who was supposed to pick me up at the ministry. Well, when they finally arrived, five helicopters windmilling there, refueling... had hoses running all over the... so you can imagine all the confusion.

Q. Was the commander of the airfield and Charlie as commander of the ground force in contact with Tehran?
A. I didn't have the radio to contact Tehran—the radio they used there was that satellite radio—and they couldn't afford one or they didn't think of me, so most of the time I didn't know what in the hell was going on. So we were waiting, waiting, waiting for decisions as to what to do. Two of the helicopters then announced that they had hydraulic problems. The flight was already less than the minimum and the idea of losing two more helicopters, Charlie had to make a decision. Then we heard shooting... and here comes the bus! Full of pilgrims. The security teams brought this bus between the planes. Some of the people on the bus could speak English. And they asked, "Who are you guys? Who are you guys?" There was a little deception story that we were supposed to have... that we were loading up Russian equipment. So, to those who spoke English we said, "We're the fucking Russians!"

Q: So that was a classic story. As I said, I hadn't heard it myself, I heard it later.
A: As we were there in this confusion, the left helicopter took off and BOOM, it hits a C-130. So my guys went up there and helped pull people out of the wrecks. And our airplane, which was untouched—yeah, we were on the fuel plane... we were riding in on those cushions of fuel. The helicopters were supposed to fill up from my plane. And there it is, the damned aircraft full of goop! So, meanwhile, there are four other helicopters wind-milling around there. And I was not able

to communicate with Charlie at this point... Demolitions, they had demolition charges. It would have taken them five minutes to blow them up, and they left everything. They left money, escape money, they left every goddamned thing there and ran away!

Q: The helicopters were sitting there still, just idle?
A: As we left they were still wind-milling. Oh hell yes, they were still running. They were still running. That's why, next morning, when Iranian fighters finally arrived, they strafed them and destroyed them on the ground; not knowing that there's nobody there except a bunch of money! And a lot of documents.

Afterwards, when we got back home, I briefed the operation to the CINCEUR, and after I finished briefing and debriefing I turned in all the equipment and all the money. All I had left was two pockets full of those damn rocks [from the Desert One crash site]. I went to CINCEUR and gave him a bunch of rocks and I gave some to other people. I was the rock man there, all over the place. So that's about it in a nutshell. That's what happened.

Later, we were sitting up there and listening to the news, and they mentioned the SF Detachment in Germany, and my guys were still there in Tehran. Lemke, McEwan weren't able to get out with us. They had to use their original program.

Q: Was there as E&E [Escape and Evasion] Plan B?
A: An E&E Plan to get back with their passports and their cover stories and everything else.

Q: So they were there on site at the embassy and the Ministry of Defense waiting for you?
A: Right, they were in Tehran living in a hotel. Then when it didn't come off, they returned back to the hotel, and, you know, said "well the whole thing is off." Meadows did have a radio so he knew the whole thing was off. So he told my guys, "The thing is off guys, get out the best you can." Which they were trying to do, but they couldn't just run to the airport and say, "Take me home." And then the Pentagon made

this statement about my guys who were still there. I could have killed that "unidentified source" at the Pentagon.

Q: During the time that this operation was going on outside the city, what were your two guys doing, your guys in the city, doing?
A: Oh, they were waiting for us at the meeting point with Meadows and the vehicles.

Q: They had the vehicles all set?
A: Oh yes, at what they called the Brick Factory. And there were some drivers there. And at one point we were going to split from "SoF." They would go to the right to the embassy and we'd go to the left to the ministry and do our stuff.

Q: Your element that was supposed to go to the ministry, how many people would that have been once they got in there?
A: We had, I actually had seven people programmed for that, plus myself.

Q: Seven plus yourself? The "SoF" element was 90?
A: Approximately. Charlie had the numbers right. It's because Charlie had a big target, and I only had three people. The intelligence on our guys in the ministry was very good. They allowed them to write letters. For some reason, they didn't take them to the embassy compound. Their letters would say, "Well from my height I could see..." He was writing this letter... they censored it, but they didn't realize that what he was saying was that from where he was on the third story on the right wing... So we knew exactly where that guy was. I talked to him later at one of the reunions, and I said, "Hey, you did a damned good job, you know." He was so clever, it was just like a spy novel, he really slipped that one over.

Q: Was he military?
A: No, he was State Department.

Q: Your fellows that were in there then, did their E&E plan work? Were they supposed to go out immediately or were they going to go out with you originally and then go out?
A: Which one, the guys inside?

Q: Yes, the guys inside.
A: Oh, the ones inside. They were inside for two months.

Q: But were they going to go out with you at the end?
A: On the exit they were going to join us and depart. Of course, like I said, since that was cut off they had to make it on their own.

Q: Did they have any problems getting out?
A: No, they had a good cover story. What helped, really, were prior departures. They said, "Well, shit, those guys were here before."

Q: They'd been in and out? Because you said they had been in a couple of times.
A: Yeah, so that was—I hadn't thought about it, but later, when you establish patterns... Well later, when you establish a pattern like that, it turned out to be very, very helpful.

Q: That's good. Instead of putting somebody in one time, you do it a couple of times, that makes sense. What was your intelligence, other than your guys, how was the intelligence sources inside Tehran? Were they making contact?
A: What do you call it, HUMINT [Human Intelligence]? None.

Q: None? Yours was the only HUMINT?
A: Yeah. Other intelligence—as far as the buildings, the compound of the embassy—it was plentiful. I don't know what company did it, but you saw a model of my area. They had a model of the entire Tehran area. That thing was a monster. I mean, the entire Tehran, everything. And of course, they mailed me only my one piece of the cake, whatever. Mine was just cut out and mailed to me for training.

Q: That must have been in a hangar then or someplace.
A: It must have cost a lot of money. Now what happened to it is a mystery. Nobody could find it.

Q: Your piece was about four foot square, if I remember.
A: Six by four. Can you imagine how big the whole city model was?

Q: What was the command relationship with you and your element with Beckwith and his "SoF" element and the guys on the ground?
A: Well, Charlie and I were co-equal commanders with equal missions, of course, I didn't have, like I said, a mission as big as Charlie. But we were equal. We were both colonels.

Q: But when it came to making the decision to pull out or abort the mission, it was his call?
A: It was his call. Well, it was actually GEN Vaught, but Charlie talked to him continuously on a satellite radio. But Charlie said, "Hey, we cannot do this."

Q: The article mentions, and this is why I refer to the *Newsweek* article here, that while six was the minimum number of helicopters that we'd said was going to be used, Charlie Beckwith, later on, said that they could probably have done it with two, and he had six in there because he thought they were going to lose birds, and he wanted to make sure he had enough to get there.
A: No, no, there's no way. We had a lot of equipment. We had scaling ladders, we could have not flown in the time that we had remaining, because we were supposed to take-off and land just at the break of dawn. So if you can imagine two American helicopters ferrying back and forth. Back and forth wouldn't have done it. What Charlie said later, when we talked, he said had we lost... had we delivered all the force, had we liberated all the guys, and by that time if we had lost all but two helicopters it would have sufficed to ferry the hostages from the football field to the airport. Just to make that jump, but not for the operation...

Q: Not to get in?
A: No, no way.

Q: You could have gotten two going out, but not to get in.
A: Right, that was the idea.

Q: Another thing the article mentions is the possibility that, because of some things that happened, there may have been some compromises inside the city. One, the Iranian fellow that was lining up the trucks and had rented the Brick Factory and all that, left a couple of days before the operation. [The interviewer is mistaken here: he is speaking of Bob Plan, an American who rented the warehouse and acquired the trucks.]
A: He did not.

Q: I'm just referring to the article. He did not? He was there all the way through?
A: He did not. He split from Meadows, because that was compromising. And he hid with his relatives a number of days. Actually, he came out way after Meadows did. [Colonel Olchovik is speaking of Fred Arooji.]

Q: It mentions in there that there was a fellow, I guess he's a CIA operative, who was in Tehran. Was there more than one? A fellow named Bob, an older guy that was in there in Tehran? Do you know who it could have been?
A: He was a member of the embassy under a cover name. Bob Plan—he was not operating. No way. [REDACTED]

Q: But these are accounts of things. It gives you a picture that there were several different elements in there, all operating more or less independently; all doing the same things. Were your guys tied in with Meadows?
A: Yes. I couldn't remember the name of that civilian guy. If they ran some sort of a net or attempted to run the net, they were all originally in the embassy itself.

Q: The obvious problem of the helicopter hitting the C-130 and causing that disaster, barring that had happened, what things were done well and what things were not done well?

A: Done well? ... I think the preparation, the rehearsals. Well, one of the things that came out of this, of course, was the whole development of the aviation arm to support counterterrorism. And the 160th...

Q: Well, I was going to say that in the preparation. And the aftermath, after everybody cried and after talking with the president and Brezinski and everybody else, they went to work and the PAVE-Low [helicopter] was an example of the development. If we had had those things in those days...

A: I would see, today, if this was a similar situation today, there would be no air/land. There would be no landing in between. It would be... Diego Garcia to Tehran non-stop and refuel on the way in.

Q: Yes... So, yes, those developments we mentioned. And I think, as far as the weaponry goes, I think we didn't come out with anything else. The most obvious shortcoming, of course, was the HUMINT. And we see that thing again in Afghanistan.

A: We're in the same boat in both times it seems like... I think so. It takes more than money to run HUMINT. You go to Harvard and say, "You're going to be a spy!" You know, you don't do that. And that's what CIA was doing. It's a good thing this is not taping... [click]

Command Sergeant Major Jeffrey Raker, Senior Enlisted Soldier, Detachment "A"

This interview is based on email exchanges between 2012 and 2015, as well as numerous conversations held between 1977 and 2018—some while the author was standing at attention in front of Sergeant Major Raker's desk.

Raker served with the 25th and 8th Infantry Divisions before volunteering for Special Forces in 1963. After completing the Qualification Course, he served with 1st Special Forces Group and completed three tours in Vietnam. He served several tours thereafter as an instructor and was qualified as a nuclear weapons release non-commissioned officer before being sent to Detachment "A" in late 1976 as the unit's senior NCO.

He brought a wealth of experience to the unit with his knowledge of unconventional warfare and counterterrorism tactics. Moreover, Raker was a consummate leader and very well respected by the men of the unit. Born in Germany prior to World War II, he was a teacher of the German language, politics, and the nuances of navigating the culture of Berlin so his men could better integrate (read "disappear") into the local community. He was also instrumental in creating a network of native Berliners to assist the unit's underground operations in the event of a war with the Warsaw Pact.

In December 1981, Raker was assigned as command sergeant major of the United States Army Institute for Military Assistance, which soon became the U.S. Army John F. Kennedy Special Warfare Center and School and ended his 30 years of service as command sergeant major of 1st SFG(A). Upon retirement, he moved to Guam with his family and became a professor at the Guam Community College.

He was inducted as a Distinguished Member of the Special Forces Regiment in 2011.

As for the Detachment's CT certification exercise, it was a three-unit affair: both "SoF" and GSG-9 were given airliners to take down, something they had both practiced ad nauseam and were able to do in their sleep, whereas we wound up with a train. Two things I recall rather vividly: prior to the actual assault our snipers had most of the bad guys in their crosshairs and had been given orders to take them out. It was shades of the Dutch train hijacking by Moluccan nationalists. It was also a scenario no one had ever practiced before. Remember our CT mission began because of the "skyjacking" threat to American airlines in Europe. In any event, we accomplished the mission and Det A was "certified."

When the Desert One fiasco happened, and the DoD spokesperson mentioned that a team of operators had been in Iran for a week under cover of European businessmen, my blood pressure went out of sight because I knew that our four guys, Clem, Scotty, Dick, and Fred, were still in-country. If the Revolutionary Guard would have had their act together, they would have been all over airports and border crossings. In the meantime I had to face Mrs. Clem daily while she was waiting for me in my living room with a sad face when I came home from work. She had, of course, figured out what Clem was up to and was the happiest wife in Berlin when I got that call from Clem that they were out and safe in Frankfurt, on their way to CONUS [Continental United States] for debriefings etc.

A piece of equipment that we did not have while we were at Hurlburt Airfield preparing for Number Two [the second rescue attempt], was a thing that looked like a big flare pistol with a two- to three-inch muzzle. Don't know what the proper name of the damn thing was, but [… we] were supposed to hold it over the locks, pull the trigger, and it would eat right through the lock. I never got to see it in action, but our team had two and "SoF" had two. When our contingent got back to Berlin, I wound up with four in my desk drawer. Corky and Colonel O had picked up "SoF's" guns off the desert floor before jumping on the tailgate of the taxiing C-130. In retrospect, I probably should have kept them rather than admitting that I had them when I received a panicked call from the Company Rep. They immediately sent their man from the American Consulate over to pick them up. He left a happy camper.

The reason Number Two [STORM CLOUD] got cancelled, by the way, was because Jack Anderson, the syndicated Columnist, had blown the cover off of it. I still suspect, as I did then, that it was a controlled leak from someone in the chain of command. There went our chance at a place in the history books. But at least we all got back alive. After our return to Berlin, Colonel O and I did not get to prepare for Christmas since we got tasked for a mission that took the two of us and Bill Durand to Ramstein and Saudi Arabia to help the Air Force thwart an attempt to take out some of their AWACS [Airborne Warning and Control System] for which Khaddafi [sic] supposedly had shed out five million bucks

Eve of the GSG-9 after-action brief in General Jack McMull's suite at the Steigenberger Hof Hotel, with Beckwith, Grimes, Colonel O, me and others in attendance, I noticed that I was out of ice for the General's Chivas that I was drinking. When I spotted a guy wearing black trousers, white shirt, red bow tie and red vest, I handed him the ice bucket and asked him to go get some ice, which he promptly did. The next morning on our way to the briefing, that guy was wearing Air Force Blues and the eagles of a full colonel. I discretely asked Stan O if he knew that that guy was a Colonel the previous night. He answered in the affirmative. To my questions as to why he didn't stop me he simply answered, "What for, Sergeant Major? You needed ice." In retrospect I have to say that the Colonel showed real class by not balking at my request and dutifully getting a bucket of ice.

Don't remember many details of Colonel Wegener (GSG-9 Commander) briefing except that I thought it was rather dry and factual (not the typical American dog and pony show), and gave a blow-by-blow account of the action. I do remember that it was pointed out the female terrorist that had herself locked into the lavatory was shot through the closed door and died from making close acquaintance with several .357 rounds. Wegener was the only one who carried a .357 magnum.

Three or four days after we came back from Florida, the Air Force asked us to assist them in a threat to take out their AWACS in Germany and in Saudi Arabia. Colonel O, Bill Durant and I deployed to Kaiserslautern in the CG's executive jet. We simply started with the assumption that the target security forces were in full compliance with all pertinent regulations. We then conducted a target analysis from the point of view of the intruder. We actually found sites where someone had left evidence of having observed take-off and landing approaches, which the Air Force then promptly covered by security personnel. They then cut orders for the three of us for Saudi, making both Bill and me

LTCs. The security at Daharan [King Abdulaziz Air Base] reflected the Saudi's awareness of a constant threat, but also several weaknesses. We got through one checkpoint that was manned by a Thai construction worker by simply exhausting my limited Thai vocabulary. That pleased him to no end and caused him to open the gate. On one occasion we were stopped by a Saudi guard who stuck an AK in our faces. Out came the IDs which did not impress him until the Colonel thought of the magic word "Askari" while pointing at each of us. That did the trick. We determined that a potential terrorist would need three days to conduct a target analysis and plan an attack. Our recommendation was to patrol all flight approaches, alternate the flight schedules, and distribute the aircraft among three bases. The AF said they would follow our advice and we asked to be flown back home.

In Kameradschaft, Jeff

Clem "Mad German" Lemke, Forward Collection Team Tehran

Lemke was another native German who sought a career in the U.S. Army and served an extended tour in Vietnam with G Company, 75th Rangers. He joined Det "A" in 1976.

Sergeant Major Lemke served more than 28 years in various Ranger and Special Operations assignments throughout his career. Beginning with an extended combat tour in Vietnam with Company G (Ranger), where he was awarded a Bronze Star with "V" and the Purple Heart, he served with Company O (Arctic Rangers) in Alaska and as an instructor with 3rd Ranger Company at Fort Benning.

He then transferred to Special Forces and was assigned to Detachment A's Team 2. While in this position, he traveled throughout East Germany and Soviet-controlled sectors to conduct sensitive collection intelligence operations. In 1979, Lemke was selected for the advanced reconnaissance team for the Iran mission; he was awarded the Defense Superior Service Medal and was personally commended by the President of the United States.

After his retirement, Lemke worked with the CIA. He was inducted into the Ranger Hall of Fame in 2021.

What follows is based on several one-on-one interviews between Lemke and the author between December 1, 2014, and January 7, 2024.

During the selection of the eventual Det Assault team, Col. O called me into his office for a one-on-one. He had a piece of paper with a bunch of names on it. I assumed he and SGM Raker had pre-selected them. He asked me one by one my opinions of the guys and if I thought they were suited for the task at hand. Well you know me, I gave him my frank opinion on each and every one of them. Somehow the word got out that I had the Col's ear. That would have been the time to get rich off the Det Members. They promised me the world if I mentioned their name. As a strange coincidence, later on as we were prepping for the second attempt out West, LTC Whittle [ex-SOF] who was in charge of our Group ["special intelligence unit"] always sought out my advice on new guys that showed up.

All my travels to Iran were with alias [REDACTED]. While acquiring the docs was a piece of cake, our guys decided that I need to go get my own visas instead of paper stamped. The first trip took me to Bonn

Advance team photograph of Iranian checkpoint, March 1980. (Courtesy of John "Scotty" McEwan)

UH-1H helo training at Mott Lake, August 1979. Bill McKeon and author. (Author's collection)

High–Standard HDM suppressed .22-caliber pistol. (Public domain)

Thermite "door opener" torch test fire. (Author's collection)

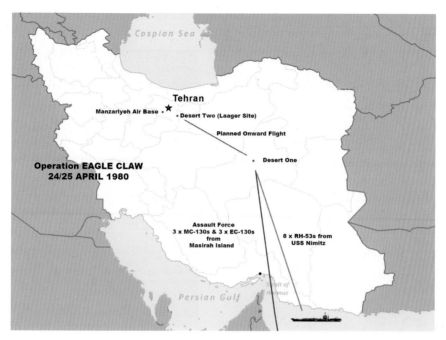

JTF-1/79 EAGLE CLAW map with insert for Desert One site. (Map by author)

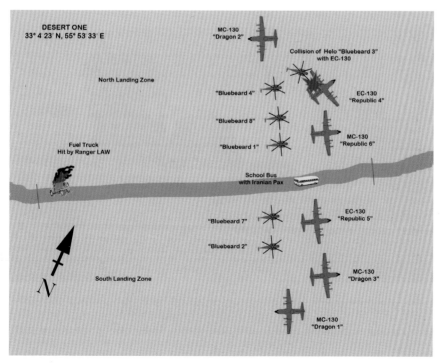

Map of the situation at the Desert One site. (Author's photo)

"How the Advanced Team handled their exit from Tehran." (In-house cartoon by Nick Brokhausen)

Staff Sergeant Stuart O'Neill decorated at end of his tour in Berlin, 1981. (Courtesy of Stu O'Neill)

President Carter speaks with the advance team at the Pentagon after the failure of Operation EAGLE CLAW, May 1980. Left to right: Clemens Lemke, Dick Meadows, Carter, General Vaught (standing with aides), Fred Arooji, John "Scotty" McEwan. (Courtesy of MG)

The Colonel's new plan after revisions.

"How Det 'A' envisioned the plan happening." (Cartoon by Nick Brokhausen)

"How Det 'A' envisioned the plan happening—1st revision." (Cartoon by Nick Brokhausen)

"We Are the Champions." Time off before deploying to Florida—winning the Berlin Brigade Football Championship, September 1980. (Author's collection)

"The Empire Strikes/Stwikes Back," Bob Hopkins and Chris Feudo en route to Florida, September 1980. "Stwikes" was used on Chris's shirt to celebrate his pronounced Italian–American accent. (Author's photo)

CPT Chris Krueger adjusts his suppressed Walther MPK, October 1980. (Author's photo)

Sergeant First Class Rick Hendricks laughing at his own joke while Tom Merrill and author feign interest, Hurlburt Airfield, October 1980. (Author's collection)

TF-158 assault force "Full Package" rehearsal flying over Eglin AFB, Florida, early November 1980—element marking stripes on rear of fuselage. (Author's photo)

OH-6 helicopter. (Public domain)

Team Three—forward security element for MFA assault. Kneeling: Werner Krueger, Howard Fedor. Standing left to right: Glen Watson, Phil Brown, John Mims, Dave Boltz, Ron Cornell. (Courtesy of Howie Fedor)

Breaktime between rehearsal flights. Corky Shelton and John Pirone, Hurlburt Airfield, November 1980. (Author's collection)

TF-158 and assault force practicing narrow road assault landings, Eglin AFB, November 1980. (Author's photo)

TF-158 readying their OH-6s for flight after off-load from transport aircraft, Hurlburt Airfield, October 1980. (Author's photo)

TF-158 assault force "Full Package" rehearsal flying over Eglin AFB, Florida, early November 1980—MH-47 C3 bird at upper edge of photo. (Author's photo)

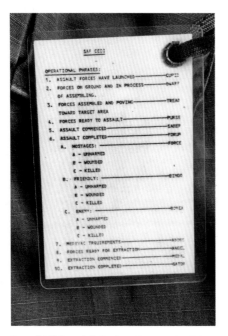

Det "A" Special Action Force CEOI—radio and call sign instructions. (Author's collection)

Sergeant First Class Ron Cornell, fully equipped for the mission, Hurlburt Airfield, October 1980. (Author's photo)

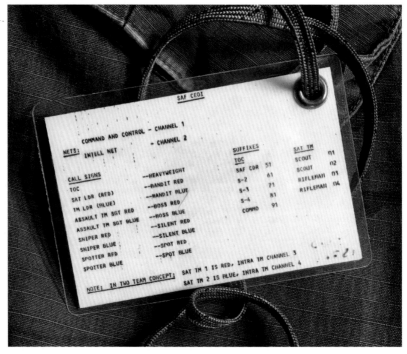

Another sample of Det "A" Special Action Force CEOI—radio and call sign instructions. (Author's collection)

Helicopter crews take a break between daylight live-fire rehearsals on Eglin AFB. (Author's photo)

AC-130 "Combat Talon" at Hurlburt Field, Florida, Hurlburt Airfield, November 1980. The gunships would be flying overhead to provide us with cover during the mission. (Author's photo)

TF–158 OH-6 with full combat load—one pilot and two assaulters, Hurlburt Airfield, October 1980. (Courtesy of Rick Hendrick)

Trial run of assault plan at Ranger Camp Rudder, Eglin AFB in daylight, November 1980. (Author's photo)

Heading home early December 1980, left to right: author, Bob Hopkins, Jon Roberts. (Author's collection)

Left to right, Ron Cornell, Howie Fedor, JJ Morrison, and Chris Krueger—small talk between practice runs with helos on Hurlbert Field. (Author's photo)

Colonel Stan Olchovik presents an end-of-tour Meritorious Service Medal award to Sergeant Major Jeff Raker in Berlin, February 1981. (Courtesy of Jeff Raker)

Helicopter exfiltration from assault of Ranger Camp Rudder, Eglin AFB in daylight, November 1980. (Author's photo)

Detachment "A"'s Commemorative Patch for JTF 1-79. (Author's collection)

where a group of Iranian student protesters had occupied the lobby of their embassy and caused a lot of ruckus. Obviously the Iranians were very uncomfortable with their presence and me on purpose pretending to pay lots of interest and attention to them. My plan worked, they spent little time checking on my docs, asked me a few questions and in no time I was back on my way to Frankfurt with my newly acquired visa.

The second trip to Geneva, Switzerland did not go as well. After arriving at the Iranian Embassy at 0900 hrs and stating my business, they took my passport and paperwork and disappeared into the back. When they prepared to close for lunch at 1200 hrs without having called me

The Lemke family's favorite photo. The "Mad German" in Vietnam with Company G, 75th Infantry (Ranger), 23 ID. (Courtesy of Clem Lemke)

I decided it was time for my evil twin Hermann to show up, I knocked forcefully on the glass partition and when a different official showed up, I demanded to know why he left me waiting for 3 hrs and acted very upset. Without as much as an apology his short response was: "Oh we forgot about you being here." He returned shortly with my PP [passport] properly stamped. I knew for a fact that they did not just forget about me, but had been checking my documents.

The fact that my passport withstood their scrutiny gave me lots of confidence for my next planned trip.

About the USMC pilots, I have nothing but disdain for that group. They should have never been part of the Mission. The Air Force's Jolly Green Giants would have been the right guys for the mission. According to Dick Meadows, during four or five rehearsals out west, only once did they do it half-assed right. The other times Dick was forced to break noise and light discipline in order to guide them into the target LZ. That was bad enough, but then came my interaction with the lead pilot/command pilot at a brief in the Pentagon after my initial recon. Part of my mission was to check out the vicinity of the Foreign Ministry in order to find the best suitable HLZs, possible obstacles and other danger areas. I gave him a run down, complete with pictures and locations of all wires in the immediate area. My parting words to him were, "you're not going to let us hang, are you?" He responded like a typical Marine: "I promise you we will get you out, no matter what." As the mission got on its way he was the first one to turn back and return to the carrier. So much for Hurrah.

Police stop: I did all the driving with the Mercedes. Scotty performed the route recon in the City (walking) while Meadows and I took a drive out to Desert Two and the warehouse. When we drove his selected route Scotty sat up front and gave me directions. Dick sat in the back. After about 10 or 15 minutes following Scotty's direction we were in a taxi/bus lane. Barriers were placed so close that vehicles were unable to enter or leave this lane. Only at intersections the barriers stopped and made it possible to turn. While waiting for the next intersection to come into view and not feeling very positive about the situation, we approached a very large intersection. My relief was very short lived, as I spotted several groups of Iranian policemen that had covered every corner of the intersection. A quick count of about twenty cops made us realize that this might not be our day. We briefly regained hope that we would escape their scrutiny, when a POV [privately owned vehicle] in front of us who was also in the wrong lane, was waved on by the closest cop. That relief did not last long as we were waved to the curb. I rolled down my window and the cop in broken English demanded to see my driver's license and passport. Confidently I reached behind my seat, searching for the familiar feel of my leather briefcase. All I came up with was Dick's legs and slightly irritated I asked him to hand me the case. While waiting for him to hand me the case I happened to look into the rearview mirror and could not help noticing that Dick's face had changed expressions, from the usually very confident to suddenly very worried. When he spoke up in a hushed voice so the cop would not be able to hear what was said he whispered that he had moved the briefcase into the trunk in order to have more room in the back seat. Still unsure why that would be much of a problem, I told him that I would hop out and retrieve it from the trunk.

While getting out of the car, my evil twin took over once more and I let the cop have it in mostly German and broken English so the cop would not get the impression that I was commending him on his uniform. My voice got louder and louder to the point of almost shouting. Knowing that he had about nineteen other cops to back him up if need be, he looked right in my face with such disdain that I expected him to slug me any minute. His eyes did not leave me and that was exactly what I wanted him to do. With a fast hand movement that would have made Houdini proud, I opened the trunk partially, just enough to pull out the briefcase and prevent him from casting a detailed look into the trunk. While this intermezzo took place, another cop (senior sergeant) stepped up to the vehicle and told the first cop to step back on the sidewalk, he had the situation in hand. Obviously I had raised so much commotion that it became embarrassing to him and he felt the need to intercede. Sensing the change in the situation I immediately calmed down and became subservient once again. He told me that driving in this lane was a minor traffic offense and I would be issued a traffic citation which I could pay before departing Iran. We all apologized profusely and with the violation in my hand and Scotty shouting out the lowered side window:

"Khomeini is great" with raised fist for emphasis, we departed the area as quickly as possible. While Dick was mostly silent and breathing deep with relief, I continued to expel my breath by chewing Scotty's ass for his unnecessary screw up. Dick knew that his action, although small and unintended, had almost caused the mission to end right there and then. He apologized in his own way, by stating that when we got stopped he literally froze and was unable to think properly. The only thing he came up with was to shoot his way out of the situation. Unfortunately there were no weapons available. He commended me on my obvious training for such a situation.

Q: Did you go back to the States before you traveled in or did you go from Frankfurt?
A: Both times the trips originated in Frankfurt. I remember meeting with a Jarhead Major from JCS in one of the departure lounges in order to sign a statement (that we are on our own—no gov connection). On his way out we told him that the ink pen we used came from you know who and the ink would disappear shortly. Never forgot the look on his face. You know Marines believe everything.

Q: You made two trips into country, about how many days were you in town on each trip? When was the first trip?
A: The first trip was in March '80, the first part I believe. Can't remember exactly how long we stayed, believe it was a week. The second time in Apr '80, we arrived four or five days before the assault force and got out about five days after the mission collapsed. My travel was with a foreign passport in a European alias.

Q: How did you meet Dick when he was in town?
A: I made contact with him at the Intercontinental. It was where the journalists stayed. Scotty stayed there as well. I stayed at the Park Hotel.

Q: The night of the infil, three of you plus drivers took the trucks out to the RON site (the night the lights didn't work on one truck). The drivers stayed with the trucks? Or did any of them come up to the site? Meadows said Fred was there with him.

A: All drivers stayed with the vehicles while us three white guys humped to the LZ. Dick was mistaken. As a matter of fact I am still convinced that Fred was not with the drivers but was already with his parents wherever they lived.

The "Mad German"'s "business" identity for travel into country. (MG)

Q: Had things worked out, you would have taken everyone to the warehouse or would you have made two trips to get everyone into town?
A: The plan called for all vehicles to travel together to a predetermined location on the edge of Tehran, at which point we were going to split up into separate forces. "SoF" was heading towards the U.S. Embassy, while Det A would have gone to the Foreign Ministry. No one would

have returned to the warehouse. As it turned out we returned all the vehicles to the warehouse before retreating to our hotels.

Q: After the mission was aborted, when did you know you had to leave? Did the radio abort message tell you or did you get another message? When did you go to Scotty's hotel?

A: We received the abort message at Desert Two, however it was so unclear and garbled that we at first assumed the mission was only delayed and we were all prepared to do this again the next 24–48 hrs. We were not told about the Chaos and Crash at Desert One while at our forward LZ. Once back at my hotel while shaving and cleaning up, I turned on my shortwave radio to *Deutsche Welle* and heard Carter talk about the mission. Needless to say I almost cut my throat shaving while listening to that SOB. I then knew we were screwed and decided to make my way to the other hotel. Normally this would have been a 15-minute taxi ride. But that morning there were no taxis to be had/seen because what seemed like a million people were flooding the streets and slowly marching towards the U.S. Embassy. Unfortunately my destination forced me to cut through the masses instead of marching with them. I did receive a few hostile looks and resorted a few times to raising my fists and shouting with the best of them. After I reached the hotel, we met together and decided to get the hell out of Dodge the best way we could. Now you know the rest of the story.

Fred Arooji, Forward Collection Team Tehran

Fred was born in Iran and immigrated to the United States where he joined the U.S. Air Force as a RF-4 "Phantom" aircraft technician. He was recruited for the Iran mission because of his native language skills, after volunteering without having any idea of the dangers involved. After the mission, his wish to become a helicopter pilot was granted and he served with the 160th Special Operations Aviation Regiment, retiring as a Chief Warrant Officer 5.

The author spoke with Fred in 2020 to discuss his role in Operation EAGLE CLAW. Other elements of the interview were from the article retrieved December 12, 2022, from USSOCOM website, at www.socom.mil/Pages/ EagleClawveteranSpecialOpsAviatorreceives2013BullSimonsAward.aspx, written by Mike Bottoms, 2013.

The hostage rescue mission in Iran became known as Operation EAGLE CLAW and the mission planners would have to bring in unique talent from throughout the Department of Defense. One skill they were looking for was Farsi language speakers.

"Shortly after the embassy in Iran had been overrun by so called students, and at that point some sixty Americans were being held hostage, we quickly found the need to have some Farsi speakers or Iranian Americans," retired Army Lt. Col. Bucky Burruss, an EAGLE CLAW participant said. "We searched DoD and one of the ones we interviewed was a young Airman named Fred Arooji and pretty quickly we recognized that he was someone special."

Born in Iran, Arooji immigrated to America as a child and enlisted in the Air Force in 1971. He was serving as an avionics mechanic for RF 4 Phantom jets when the call came out for Farsi language speakers. Intrigued, Arooji went through the interview process not knowing the reason DoD was looking for Farsi speakers. Making it through the interview process, Arooji was selected for EAGLE CLAW.

"I went through all kinds of training, and months later General James Vaught (overall EAGLE CLAW mission commander) called me in his office and asked me 'Are you ready to travel?'" Arooji said. "I said yes and he said 'Okay son, go and get your tickets to Tehran.'"

"It was decided that we needed to send in an advance party to do last-minute reconnaissance and Fred, as a native Iranian, had the tongue, had the eyes, the ears, and had the sense of things happening in Iran, so we asked him to be part of the advanced party," said retired Army Captain Wade Ishimoto, EAGLE CLAW planner.

Vaught would be the overall commander, but the commander on the ground would be Special Operations legend Army Colonel Charles Beckwith. Arooji's first meeting with Beckwith was testy.

"I was with Captain Bucky Burruss one day and Colonel Beckwith walks in the room, big guy, huge, he had a real raspy voice," Arooji said. "He looked at me and said, 'That beard, that looks good, don't shave that beard.'"

"Colonel Beckwith turned to walk away, stopped and looked at me and said 'I'll tell you what son, while you're here, you keep your mouth shut, you understand?' I said, 'Yes I do.' He looked at me again and said 'No, you don't understand, this is my country, I love my country, and I am not going to let any son-of-a-bitch destroy it, so you keep your damn mouth shut while you are here and if I ever find out you are talking too much I'll put you in a jail or you will never see the sun again.'"

Arooji continued, "I stepped two or three feet toward Colonel Beckwith, I looked him straight in the eye and told him, 'Sir, you know what the difference is between you and me?' He said, 'What is it?' I said, 'the difference is you were lucky, you were born in this country as an American, I earned mine and I love it just as much as you do. 'He looked at me and said, 'We'll see,' and turned and walked away. I thought I was going to faint. Bucky turns to me and says 'Hey Freddy, he really likes you.'"

Later that day, according to Arooji, Beckwith would approach him in the chow hall and give him a big hug and tell him "You know what, you are a true American."

Arooji joined another Special Operations legend, Army Major Dick Meadows, for the reconnaissance mission in Iran ahead of EAGLE CLAW and where they encountered significant challenges for which Arooji's ingenuity would prove to be invaluable.

"The mission was supposed to occur on the night of April 24th and 25th, 1980. That particular day, the 24th of April, Dick Meadows and Fred went by the warehouse where the vehicles were stored and Fred saw that a ditch had been dug across the driveway. That was significant and there was no way those vehicles could be driven out," Ishimoto said.

"Dick said, 'Man what are we going to do?' and about ten or fifteen feet away there were kids playing soccer, so I said to Dick we need to give these kids a basket of oranges and I then asked the kids to help me move some concrete chunks into the ditch and they did," Arooji said.

The ditch repaired, Meadows and Arooji waited for the rescue mission to unfold. Unfortunately, the hostage rescue mission was aborted when a helicopter collided with a C-130 killing eight servicemen at the Iranian staging area known as Desert One.

"After the mission failure, the media splashed that there were Americans of Iranian descent involved with the mission inside Tehran—this put Fred under great danger," Ishimoto said.

"We had no idea what took place. I dropped Dick off at his hotel and I got back to my hotel and I turned the TV on and I see they are carrying the bodies of the individuals that got burned and the crash site burning, so I am in deep trouble at this point," Arooji said.

Arooji then went back to Meadows' hotel and took him to the airport.

"We had a Mercedes someone had provided us, so Dick told me, 'Take the Mercedes and head to the Turkish border and we'll contact you there,'" Arooji said. "Well as it turned out, the keys to the Mercedes were in the pocket of another gentleman and he was on his flight home. The only way in and out of Iran now was through Tehran."

"We had no contact with him after the mission was aborted," Ishimoto said. "I frankly thought I would never see Fred Arooji alive again."

Arooji would spend a harrowing two weeks under the constant pressure of being caught before he safely made his way back to the United States.

"When Fred got back he was still an Airman in the United States Air Force," said retired General Richard Cody, former vice chief of staff of the U.S. Army and commander of the 160th Special Operations Aviation Regiment. "When he got back to the United States President Carter wanted to meet him, and at that meeting President Carter said,

'Young man, I believe I have just met one of the bravest of young men in uniform.'"

"After I had received my award for the mission, President Carter asked me what my wishes were and I said I wanted to be a military pilot," Arooji said.

Lieutenant Vaught would work to ask the Air Force to grant Arooji an inter-service transfer to the Army where he would become a Special Operations helicopter and fixed-winged pilot. Time would prove he was a natural and born to fly.

Stuart "Stu" O'Neill, MFA Assault Team Member

Stu joined Det "A" as the junior engineer (demolitions) sergeant on Team 6 in 1978, coming from ODA-222 in the 10th Group. He was renowned as the "most Irish" guy in the unit and had a running debate battle going on with "Scotty" McEwan (the most Scottish guy in the unit) over the Troubles in Northern Ireland. Following his tour with Det "A," he joined the USAF as a Counterintelligence Officer. He was on the first INF Treaty Verification Team based in Votkinsk USSR, 1988–1991 and then on the first START Team in Pavlograd, Ukraine, in 1995. Stu also stood up and commanded the USAF Anti-Terrorism Team (AST) in 1997. Upon retirement he had served with both the FAA and TSA.

This section is based on interviews and correspondence between O'Neill and the author, 1977–2024.

By 1979, Detachment "A" was becoming a fully dual mission unit. In addition to the normative UW stay behind mission which had originally driven the creation of the unit back in 1956, Det A became more and more adept at its other mission of CT. Through internal training at ranges within the city and training with other units like the German SEK and British SAS, members of the Det were the primary CT unit for the U.S. Army within EUCOM. The unit's 12Bs [engineer sergeants] set up various shooting ranges once the weather improved sufficiently to consistently use them. Also employed were old, underground German army ranges right on Andrews Kaserne. Members of the six A-Teams in the detachment put thousands of rounds downrange each day. The primary firing techniques that were taught were CQB instinctive firing with handguns and aimed rapid fire with shoulder-fired weapons.

The Detachment was required to undergo a certification before it was deemed to be operational as a CT unit for the U.S. Army. The exercise was conducted in West Germany and the scenario was a train being taken over by terrorists and the recovery of the rail asset by Detachment A members. This objective was somewhat different from the usual house/ room clearing and aircraft takedowns that the Detachment members had practiced ad nauseam. It was not long after this exercise that the Det started looking at events in the Shah's Iran. As Iran spiraled into the revolutionary abyss in 1978, the Det was already in discussions within EUCOM for potential deployment to protect sensitive U.S. assets located within the soon-to-be Islamic Republic. These discussions did not result in a deployment of the Detachment members, but had some influence in later discussions which commenced after November 4, 1979.

As the detachment was a multi-purpose unit, primarily focusing on the UW and CT missions, this on many occasions would lead to potential operational stresses on the detachment due to conflicting requirements.

On November 4, 1979, Iranian militants representing themselves as students came over the fence at the massive U.S. Embassy complex in downtown Tehran. And planning for the mission began. It became quickly clear that the mission objective would be very simple, the execution of the mission would not be. One of the issues that perplexed planners in the initial days were the distances involved. It was finally determined that the ground mission in Tehran would be split between "SoF" assets who would go over the wall at the embassy complex and the Detachment team that would rescue the three members of the embassy staff that were being held at the Foreign Ministry.

As the planning cycle extended through late winter and early spring it became evident that the Det members would likely be able assist in a mission set beyond assaulting the Foreign Ministry. Since the beginning of Special Forces, a premium had been placed on bringing men into Special Forces who had language ability; a high premium had been placed on those with native ability and those who had either spent time in potential target countries or especially those who had grown up there. Legislation passed by Congress, particularly the Lodge Act, which offered a quicker path to U.S. citizenship, also brought into the U.S. Army a variety of Eastern European recruits who would potentially be excellent A-Team members. This long-term recruiting of military personnel from other nations would prove to have been both fortuitous and vital to EAGLE CLAW's preparations.

By 1979, the CIA's Directorate of Operations was a shadow of its former self. Twin hits of nearly 40% personnel reductions had decimated and demoralized the directorate. This left the agency with little [REDACTED] to assist in the execution of a hostage rescue of two separate groups within Tehran and the furtherance of moving assault elements from what would become Desert Two into Tehran to execute the actual freeing of the embassy personnel.

DoD planners came to the conclusion, more of a reality, that this deficit of ground intelligence assets would have to be made up by DoD itself. After it was determined that at least two of the detachment members, one from the UK and the other from the European continent, could be of use on the ground in Iran well prior to the arrival of the members of EAGLE CLAW, it now turned out that Detachment A would not only be involved in a potential hostage rescue, it would have two missions within the rescue plan, one at the Foreign Ministry and a larger part securing the actual intelligence to allow planners to finalize their efforts and then to assist the assault forces on the ground to get from Desert Two (the hide site southeast of Tehran) into the city of Tehran proper. Detachment A would have a very busy spring.

Until General Vaught stood up in an Egyptian aircraft hangar on April 23 and announced that the plan to rescue was just that, a plan. Because the mission plan had not yet been approved, the Detachment was required to maintain not only the CT training but also its core UW mission, which was not going away because of a mission that may or may not be a "go"—no matter how significant.

In the 1970s the Cold War was still in full swing. To counter the Soviet threat, the Special Operations world conducted an exercise called FLINTLOCK during which forces from the U.S. and other nations would jump, swim, helo and walk into simulated targets in Europe. It was a huge undertaking from a planning, logistics and transportation standpoint. The Det played a large role in every iteration of the exercise. Significant in the spring of 1980 was the fact that this one event would task three of six of the Detachment's A-Teams just when it needed to be able to look at every team member it had for possible Iran deployment. This year Teams One, Three and Five were dedicated to the exercise. Membership in Team One consisted of Vietnam veterans, many of whom had served in Studies and Observations Group projects like CCC and CCN. Team Five was also one of the better units in Berlin and had coalesced into a younger version of Team One with a highly effective team sergeant and team membership. Team Three, the unit's SCUBA team, also had strong members who wanted in on the Iran mission. Because of the exercise, these team members were not available for Iran.

It became a difficult task to select a team for possible Iran deployment. Two teams had given up members to the Det's Iranian intelligence gathering role and Team Six was also short due to recent rotations out. Early in the internal planning cycle it became apparent that the Berlin team that would go down range would be an ad hoc element that would be put together from Teams Two, Four and Six for the Iran mission only. It now came down to how to select the members of this unit, this on top of everything else that Colonel O and CSM Raker had to do.

It was only natural that the commander of Detachment A, Colonel Stan Olchovik, in concert with Army leadership would lead the operation. There would be no medics on the team, this due to constraints on the number of personnel who would go forward and the presence of medical personnel within other ground elements that would be present.

Probably one of the most important decisions on team composition was that of who would be the senior NCO. The detachment had no shortage of strong leaders in this area, especially in the Master Sergeant and Sergeant First Class ranks. For Raker and Olchovik it was imperative that this NCO would be one that could efficiently form this recently created unit into an effective team and then train the team to go forward. Sergeant 1st Class Corky Shelton was chosen for this role.

For the rest of the team, different members were selected in different and diverse ways. An intense, two-week Close-Quarter Battle course was held with the top finishers being assured of potential Iran team slots. But the top two finishers in this contest were both from Team Five, which effectively put them out of the running. While the top two finishers were to be excluded due to their duties for the FLINTLOCK exercise, the number three finisher from Team 6 would be chosen for Iran. The final team that would leave from Tempelhof Airfield on 19 April would include one member from Team One, two from Teams Four and Six, and three from Team Two. By military specialty [MOS] most of the team members were weapons specialists; with two engineers (this would be significant later).

Now they would wait, as the timeline was a complete unknown. All their equipment would be off-the-shelf and the training schedule was, at best, fluid. The advantage that the new element had was that all the skill sets that would be necessary to the successful mission completion once on the ground were ones at which the element members were very adept,; moving, shooting, communicating, breaching, room clearing, rappelling, and high-speed driving were second nature to anyone who had spent time in Det A.

In early April, members of the element were assembled in the Detachment's second floor conference room and informed of their selection and informed of their mission: the successful liberation and exfil to the soccer stadium of the three embassy staff from the Iranian Foreign Ministry.

The three had been at the Foreign Ministry on November 4 and had been kept there since. Their conditions of confinement were significantly different from those at the embassy, for several days after the sack of the embassy they had maintained an open phone line with Main State in Washington, D.C., but they were prisoners nonetheless.

The Iran element members were also informed that they did not have to worry about how they would get into Iran or Tehran, or for that matter how they would get out of the country. Their focus should only be on cracking the Foreign Ministry nut.

The first decision that had to be made was how to actually get the three members of the embassy staff, including Bruce Laingen, out of the Foreign Ministry where they were being held (which was conveniently located across the street from a police station) to the stadium where all of the hostages would be exfiltrated to the then secured, Mehrabad Airport.

This was the point of discussion for the first several days with a variety of options being examined. Everything from rappelling from the roof (how do we get on the roof?) to tossing grenades in the windows (we didn't yet know in which room or rooms the hostages were being held) to the final idea, which was also the simplest: Drive up to Foreign Ministry, get out of the vehicle, walk up to and into the building and take the hostages out. The feeling went at the time that if the team had the element of surprise it should take a few seconds or minutes for those securing the hostages to react, by which time the team would already have the hostages or have a significant advantage in firepower. If the team didn't have the element of surprise, they were fucked.

Soon into the planning process a package arrived at the Detachment from the U.S.; the Intelligence Community (IC) had been nice enough to build a mock-up of the target area of the Foreign Ministry. This proved to be very beneficial in the planning process. That said, there was a dearth of intelligence or any real information as to the activity around the Foreign Ministry, how many people were assigned to the ministry, how many would be there at the target time (late at night) and how the facility was secured. Initially, team members were also woefully uninformed as to how many men were assigned to the police station across the street and their armaments. For all of the IC's emphasis on non-HUMINT assets over the past several years the team was not getting much in the way of satellite imagery Information from the advanced team would fill in many of the gaps later.

Initial work on formulation of a way to get the three Americans out of the Foreign Ministry and to the stadium was hammered out by the team. Corky Shelton led the effort for the most part Colonel O was spending more and more time in Stuttgart and the U.S. working with other unit leaders and DoD planners. More esoteric plans like rappelling down the sides of the Foreign Ministry and others fell by the wayside until a more direct approach was formulated. The team would approach in multiple vehicles, exit adjacent to the Foreign Ministry and then go by foot into the Foreign Ministry building itself, enter and secure the hostages. If necessary breaching charges would be used on secured entry points. All this would be done as quickly as possible, with as much surprise and as little fanfare allowable. Guards would be neutralized and element members would also be set up to put fire onto the nearby police building and any responders as necessary. As soon as the hostages exited the building and once into the vehicles, all the members would reassemble to the vehicles and drive to the soccer stadium where they would link-up with the others for helicopter exfiltration to the airport. The plan was simple and also contingent on the fact that they would not be greeted by a large force guarding the three in the ministry. Nine men with small arms would not be at a good start point against a prepared and heavily armed force. The team members had received intelligence that indicated that those, if any, present would be few in number, inexperienced and lightly armed. That was about one of the few pieces of good news the Berliners got before departing the city.

Before movement to Egypt, the Berlin element had a team, had a plan and finally, had to wait. At the end of each duty day in April as team members nailed down a plan and then fine-tuned it and gathered necessary equipment, they would return home not knowing when or even if the mission would go. There was still a large contingent of people from the NCA on down who thought that the mission would not be a go. Many thought that the President would never approve the operation and that all efforts were just a contingency in case the "students" started killing the hostages. When the word came down to go forward to Egypt for final mission prep many within even the Iran Element itself thought that the mission would in all likelihood be scratched.

As April progressed issues within Iran itself seemed to be coming to a head, more talk of imminent trials or tribunals for the hostages seemed to come from the revolutionary leadership. Every day in between training and prep a discussion occurred as to whether the team would go forward or not. Each night as team members would depart the conference room/ mission prep area team members would joke about how many minutes of sleep they would get that night.

Early in the third week of April 1980, Colonel O returned from a trip to meet with command. After his arrival that morning he had all of the team members as well as the other members of the whole detachment not tasked with FLINTLOCK duties assemble in the third-floor hallway for an announcement. He as well as the unit CSM came up the stairs and then standing in front of the assembled group, announced that the Iran team would be going forward to their jump off point. To this extent the mission was a go. The element didn't know if they would be going to Iran, but they were sure as hell leaving Berlin.

On the afternoon of April 19 the Iran element members moved by vans to the U.S. Air Force terminal at Tempelhof Airport. As the team members moved though the city traffic in the Detachment's civilian Ford Transit vans, each member went through mental checklists ensuring that he had each item needed. While most were sure that they had forgotten some essential item, in most cases they probably hadn't. The list was short, each member carried a 9mm Walther MPK with as many loaded mags he could carry; each man also carried at least one pistol, a 9mm Walther P-38. Most also carried a suppressed .22 cal High Standard HD pistol as well and—in true SF fashion—most also carried at least one knife. The team didn't carry rucksacks or a lot of food or water. The team was ready for one night's work in Tehran and little else.

In Egypt the Det members did their final mission prep and the leadership met with other unit commanders to iron out final details. Since the unit had not been involved in mission rehearsals and had only leadership level involvement in planning there was a lot to do. The days were long with waiting and everyone was impatient for word as to the status of our mission.

The overall plan was set: C-130s would depart Egypt carrying the ground elements to eventually land at a site called Desert One, there they would marry up with rotary wing assets from the Navy, CH-53s, one of the few active birds that could make the long distance flight into Desert One, from the USS *Kitty Hawk* in the Gulf. Before the mission could continue, the eight helos would have to be refueled on the ground, before they could carry the ground units to Desert Two. There they would RON and then move out the next night to Tehran to complete the mission.

On April 24 all of the men assembled to hear a last pre-mission brief by General Vaught and then moved to the aircraft. The hostages had been taken on November 4 and now the United States was going to get them back. By this time, the Det A team had changed configuration. A 7-man MFA assault element would fly on one of the Special Ops birds, while two (O'Neill and Cooper) would fly on a fuel bird as part of the security team for Desert One. Their aircraft was overloaded by about ten thousand pounds beyond its wartime max weight.

There have been many descriptions of what Desert One was like as various USAF and Navy aircraft landed while at around the same time an Iranian tour bus wandered by and was stopped by the road team and its passengers detained. In the area as well was at least one fuel truck which was hit by a Light Anti-tank (LAW) rocket, the driver of the truck quickly exited the burning vehicle and made Olympic time in moving to a following vehicle. Needless to say, it was not as organized as it was planned to be. The scene was a cross between a 1980s Hollywood disaster epic and a low-budget action flick. There were burning fuel trucks and tourist buses and there was waiting. A lot of waiting at Desert One.

As the night drew into early morning, the CH-53s got more and more behind schedule as the daylight line was passed, the men at Desert One still awaited the remaining helos. Finally what would be the last bird arrived at Desert One. In the meantime operators gathered gear, awaiting orders to load. What most on the ground did not know was that two of the eight birds were not coming in at all; one had turned back to the aircraft carrier and another had set down in the face of a haboob, a swirling wall of sand that defied the helos and their air filters to try and make it through. When the final Navy bird set down they were quickly asked to exit and meet with leadership gathering nearby. The final arrival meant that there were six operational helos ready to move forward to Desert Two. Shortly after the bird set down, and leadership met, the order was finally given to load up—the reach of the U.S. military was moving closer to Tehran and the hostages. What the men loading onto the '53s did not know was that there was significant consternation as to the suitability of the recently landed helicopter.

The Marines flying that final bird announced their bird wouldn't be leaving Desert One and the number now was five, one short of the required six. There would have to be discussions on this development and leadership did just that. As those moving forward continued to load and check their gear, they would soon get another order once the leadership conclave was concluded.

In the confusion of the evening and early morning there were conflicting instructions passed down and due to the scattered disposition of the aircraft and thus the scattered pockets of people milling around waiting for the helicopters to show. The helos that showed up first were fueled up first and thus were ready for loading by the operators who were ready to get going. Soon after the arrival of the final Navy helo, the instruction was passed to load the helos, but that order was given before the leadership group got together to decide the disposition of the final aircraft and thus to in fact decide the fate of the mission.

Then the orders changed to unload the helos and reload the C-130s. The leaders at Desert One had met, discussed the situation, and spoken to Washington and the President. The decision was made with the NCA that the mission would be scrubbed for at least that night. Those on the ground could feel the air go out of the mission, everyone maintained their professionalism, but the disappointment was palpable. People moved their gear back to fixed-wing aircraft and then the equipment was loaded back and men boarded the birds to leave. It was necessary to move the now non-critical rotary wing craft so the C-130s could head back to Egypt. Most members of the Det were standing clear as the aircraft were being marshalled about the central area of Desert One.

While one helo was being directed to lift off and shift, dust kicked up, and the helo then seemed to slide into a C-130 to its front. Sparks kicked up as the rotors tore into the fixed wing bird. The first inkling that something was wrong was the noise we heard: a loud "whomp" that reverberated through the area. Some would later say that it sounded like the area was taking mortar fire.

After the helo collided with the C-130, disorder reigned for several minutes as those people in the aft area of the affected Hercules quickly exited the aircraft and moved away. Many of the operators assisted those aircrew who had been injured in the explosion which would claim the lives of eight of the personnel, three Marines and five USAF C-130 crew. Det members also aided the injured and assisted them to the remaining fixed wing aircraft. As people were counted and a check was made of the area, the last of the C-130s started to move to ready for take-off.

On the flight out of Desert One one of the C-130s carrying about half the Berliners hit a low wall shortly after take-off. The situation on the aircraft was tenuous with wounded moaning and periodically screaming in pain. Det members were assisting the "SoF" medics in caring for the wounded whose injuries in many cases approached severe and ranged from there. Rumors started in that aircraft that the wall strike would result in the aircraft having to ditch in waters which caused even more consternation. Needless to say the USAF bird did not have to ditch and made it all the way to Oman without further incident.

The aircraft all landed in Oman and discharged the wounded before taking off for the final leg back to their point of origin. After the wounded were taken off the aircraft, each of the planes were shrouded in near total quiet beyond the constant drone of the four engines as they made their way to Egypt. Aircrew, Det members and everyone else were all intermingled on the flight back, still not saying a word.

As the aircraft landed back at the base, the Det members as well as the others filed quietly off the aircraft and into the main hangar. Everyone gathered around, General Vaught once again spoke to the assemblage, this time of course with a much different message.

For the next two days Det members loitered around the Egyptian base talking to other ground element members from FT Bragg and each other, but still not really saying all that much, when it came down to it they were really just waiting for a ride back to the city. Other units went back to Florida and Ft Bragg. Navy personnel returned home as well. The Berliners had the shortest commute, and would head back to Germany in one flight leg.

Berlin

The flight back to the city was again quiet and the men landed at the U.S. military terminal and got on the same vans that had taken them to Tempelhof less than 10 days earlier from Andrews Kaserne. After arriving back at the Det the returning Berliners stowed weapons and inventoried equipment, figuring out just exactly what had been inadvertently left on the floor of the Iranian Desert. The Iran team were greeted with questions about the op, but not too many, and in hushed tones.

Two days later the team met with Colonel Olchovik and were debriefed about the operation. After that the Iran unit was given a week off and most spent the next several days in various states of inebriation, trying to get the smell of burning flesh out of their nostrils.

Det A would have a significantly larger and much more integrated role in the next phase of the hostage rescue effort. The second mission team members would this time be involved in all aspects of the rehearsal and spend a substantial amount of time in the U.S. prepping to return once again for the Americans.

The second mission was never launched.

Jim "OC" O'Callahan, MFA Assault Team Member

Born in 1944, Jim enlisted in the U.S. Army, served in Vietnam, and retired as a Special Forces Chief Warrant Officer. A member of the 10th Special Forces group, he was selected for Detachment "A" and joined the unit in 1978. He received the Ranger School Darby Award at the age of 36.

At the time of the Iran hostage taking, he was the Senior Engineer (demolitions) Sergeant on Team 2 and was selected for the mission as one of two engineers with the MFA assault team.

This interview is based on a letter from "OC" to the author written in March 2014.

In 1979, the main news on America's mind was gas prices, watching the Americans beat the Russians in Hockey, and the Iranian Hostage situation. All the guys in the Det were waiting for someone to do something. The days went by in a dreary progression with nothing happening.

We were near Berchtesgaden doing winter warfare training, when several members were called out and disappeared. This immediately started rumors flying throughout the unit. Our team returned to Berlin. A few days after Colonel "O" called several individuals into the unit classroom, briefed us about the mission after he read the secrecy agreement we all had to adhere to.

He then gave everyone a chance to decline. This was the most important thing that the Unit had done in a while. Excitement was high, and everyone was wondering what were the criteria for being selected. We were released from the meeting with a warning not to discuss what the meeting was about. The secrecy lasted for about ten minutes. There were capable, disappointed and angry men, who were not chosen. None of us ever learned what the criteria were. We were just happy to be selected.

Our mission was to free three diplomats being held in the Ministry of Foreign affairs. We received a huge tabletop diorama of the area around the target. All of the buildings, roads, etc. were there, and the studying began. With a mission statement and the very detailed diorama, the mission plan began to unfold. The target was on a tree-lined street. The Iranian Officers' Club was across the street and ran parallel to the

Ministry of Foreign Affairs (MFA). At the end of the street there was a "T" intersection which housed elements of the National Police.

We began mornings with a meeting, and then hours of shooting at the underground range located at Andrews Barracks. Our primary weapons included suppressed High Standard HDM .22 pistols. And all became very proficient. Shooting was for speed and accuracy. We also had MPK submachine guns and a couple of M-16s. Days ended with physical training.

Extensive training was necessary, especially at night because assets in Iran had secured an automobile, and a Volkswagen van. The mission was to happen at night, so we practiced driving with and without headlights. We also practiced shooting at targets while on the move from our vehicles.

A plan was being hammered into shape. It needed a lot of revision, so we kept working on it. One of the problems was that requirements kept changing, but we adapted to them. We continued to receive intel all the way up to time we launched and by the time we left for Iran, we had the plan for the mission ironed out. The married guys went home for their last night. I spent the night guarding the diorama. Then it was time.

The Final Plan

The final plan was that we were supposed to drive up to an entry at the end of the MFA. This was the access point which offered the easiest access to the hostages. It was usually guarded by four sentries. There was a guard house at the entrance where the off-duty guards were located. "Sam" would step out of the car, and say something in Arabic. I was wearing a suit and got out of the other front door. Our task was to eliminate the sentries. John Mims was supposed to go with us to the guard house to make sure there were no more sentries inside. Billy Krieger was to go to the back of the van, and cover the part of the street to the rear. OC had the radios and the M-16 to hold off anyone coming from the area in front of the car and van. The Colonel, Bob Kuenstle, Corky, John Mims, and I were to force their way into the building itself and take the out the hostages with them. After this, we were supposed to drive to a soccer field near the rear of the MFA, where a Marine helicopter was tasked to pick us up and fly us to the exfil airfield.

Heading to Iran

Heading for Iran. We were dropped off at Tempelhof to wait for our flight to Wadi Kena, Egypt. A picture was taken of the group. We look businesslike. Actually that was the second picture. In the first one we were holding ice cream cones and laughing. The rest of the flight was serene, and we landed. Our first task was to meet Col. Beckwith. He handed us a beer and talked to us. We were quartered in another airplane hangar, away from "SoF." The time was spent rehearsing our plan. We were there a couple of days. We ran into friends in "SoF" who we knew in the Special Forces battalions.

On the day before we were scheduled to go in, an Airborne Ranger Company arrived. They were impressive. Every movement for getting situated was orchestrated. Everyone knew where they were supposed to go and went there with no confusion. Their Company Commander, Captain Grange (who later became a General) was in my Ranger class. I walked up to see him. His first sentence was "Ranger 'O' are you in the CIA now?" He looked shocked at my appearance, long hair, running shorts, etc.

On the Way

The next day we boarded an airplane which took us to Masirah Island off Oman. We deplaned with our equipment and settled down for the rest of the day. It was sweltering under the canvas where we waited. We had several options, sleep or talk or stare at the oil rigs. There were also the ever-present warm cokes and other warm sodas. As it became dark, we boarded the transport that would take us into a land full of people who did not like us very much. I fell asleep lying on a mattress on the deck, and awakened just before we were ready to land.

Our first task was to unload camouflage nets for the helicopters that were coming for us. The next chore was to take our personal gear (rucks, etc.). Every action was smoothly performed with speed and precision. All we could do at that point was wait.

A busload of Iranian civilians had the misfortune to be riding on a bus that came to where we were staging. A man came into view, and my impression of him was that he was the biggest, meanest-looking Ranger

I had ever seen. He was covering the petrified bus riders with an M-60 that looked like a toy in his hands. Suddenly there was a mushroom cloud-like explosion from down the road. The road watch team had blown up a fuel truck.

We stood with the others who loaded on our helicopters with us to take us nearer to Tehran. The helicopters arrived, but there were too few then were needed to take us to our objective. The president cancelled the mission. With a small amount of grumbling, we gathered behind the C-130 that was supposed to exfiltrate us back to safety. The C-130s were lined up abreast so the helicopters could refuel.

It was a very cold night, and we were freezing and wanted to get out of the cold. The pilot would not let us board. So we stood there complaining and watched the plane next to us refuel a helicopter. The chopper was finished fueling but there was what appeared to be a problem. Instead of backing away from its fueling with the C-130 plane it drifted forward and collided, just behind the port-side wing. There was an explosion, and the troops who were on the plane ran off it as if it was something they did every day. No panic at all. Flames were reaching out up to the sky and near to the other planes.

We had not been allowed to board our plane while they were fueling. We had all been whining about that, and how lucky they were when their pilot let them out of the cold during the refueling. We changed our minds about how lucky we were not to be on that bird. Within a few minutes, our airplane, and all the other planes disappeared. Things did not look good if we were left in that situation. Corky Shelton and I were standing together wondering what was going to happen. Corky said something about being stuck in the middle of Iran. We each figured out how many rounds we had if we had to fight. Corky looked at me and giving a bad imitation of Butch Cassidy said, "Those Mother Fuckers are in a lot of trouble."

As we waited we heard the sound of airplanes. They had returned to pick us up. They had taxied away to get clear of the fire. Even in that short time there was a moment for heroism. Stu O'Neill and Chris Able rescued at least one pilot from the flaming helicopter. Both earned the Soldier's Medal. On the flight out I watched Keith Perdue treat the injured. He looked like a doctor who did it every day. Professional, no stress.

The flight back was very subdued. We landed and immediately began getting our things together. We did not have much to pack so we were finished quickly.

Col. Beckwith called everyone together, and gave an impromptu after action report on his perception of what happened.

We left for an almost silent flight back to Ramstein airbase. We deplaned with all our equipment into more bitter cold weather. There were a number of men in civilian clothes walking around.

A C-130 landed. The pilot came to give us a flight briefing. He was a one-star general. His co-pilot was either a one-star or a full colonel. All the enlisted men were the equivalent of Sergeant Majors, or Master Sergeants. Another strange thing is that Tempelhof was usually closed for flights at night, but it was open for us. We had not eaten since breakfast. As soon as we took off they issued us all two meals, which we demolished.

Major Wise was waiting for us at Tempelhof to take us back to Andrews. We were quickly in our trucks and having a beer. We had returned.

The impossible had happened. The mission had failed through a series of random mishaps.

VR [Very Respectfully]

OC

Endnotes

Introduction

1   Initially, 67 people were captured, 14 of whom were released early, and 53 of whom were held for the entire 444-day-long hostage-taking.

Chapter 1, A Short History of Detachment "A" Berlin (39th Special Forces Detachment)

1   HHC, USAG, was known as 7781st Army Unit (7781AU) until late 1957.
2   U.S. Army General Orders No. 263, September 1, 1965.
3   The unit's wartime mission was assigned by U.S. Army Europe Operational Plan 4304, which is described in detail in the book *Special Forces Berlin: Clandestine Cold War Operations of the US Army's Elite, 1956–1990*, Oxford: Casemate.
4   Like the Bureau, GSG-9 was using revolvers as their service sidearm at the time, whereas Det "A" was using automatic pistols as their sidearm.
5   There were no CT specialists in the United States at the time so, as with its urban unconventional warfare mission, the men of Det "A" became the subject matter experts.
6   The Walther P-38's alloy frame was prone to breakage and not suitable for CT operations. It was replaced with the Walther P-5 in 1978.
7   The appendices on the "History of CQB" and a "CQB Training Plan" outline the starting point and underlying philosophy of the Detachment's marksmanship and Close-Quarter Battle program.

Chapter 2, Where It Began: Tehran, November 4, 1979

1   Jimmy Carter, *Keeping Faith: Memoirs of a President*, New York: Bantam Books, 1982, 461.
2   Much of the Pentagon's planning process was not visible to the members of Det "A" because of its distance from the "flagpole." It is covered well in Rod Lenahan's

book *Crippled Eagle: A Historical Perspective of U.S. Special Operations, 1976–1990*, Charleston: Narwal Press, 1998.

3   COMJTF OPLAN: "Rescue of American Hostages From AMEMB Iran" (declassified document online), available at http://www.dod.mil/pubs/foi/International_security_affairs/iranian_hostage_crisis/536.pdf accessed January 1, 2015. (Washington, D.C.: Headquarters Joint Task Force, February 26, 1980), 1A29.

4   The acronym and words "SoF," "Special Operations Forces," and "Special Forces" replace unit designations originally used throughout the manuscript which were redacted by DoD. The replacements are amended exactly as stipulated by DOPSR.

Chapter 3, Clem & Scotty

1   Bob Plan left the country days before the mission was to be executed.

Chapter 5, The Ground Force Prepares

1   FLINTLOCK was a sub-exercise within REFORGER to test Special Forces elements in Europe.

2   Colonel "O" asked Clem to review the names he and the SGM had chosen for the mission and to give his opinion about their suitability for the mission. When it became known that he had the boss's ear, every man promised Clem the world if he would mention their name.

3   Laingen was permitted a telephone call to the State Department in Washington, D.C., on April 16 that indicated they had been moved and gave their new location.

4   The information ostensibly obtained from the Pakistani cook in the embassy was revealed by the CIA during the early morning of April 23, 1980, prior to mission launch. It was later revealed that the cook was not the real source.

Chapter 6, The Advance Team's Second Insert

1   Scotty remembered this differently, saying Meadows also stayed at the Intercontinental.

2   Clem never did pay the ticket and it sits in his personal "war room" at home. Before the mission, Raker had predicted Clem might hang from a lamppost in Tehran if he got caught. Clem's response was: *"Unkraut vergeht nicht"* ("Weeds are hard to kill").

Chapter 7, From Egypt to Masirah

1   CH-47s were discussed but rejected because they would look out of place on the deck of an aircraft carrier. They would be a clear indicator of what was planned to any enemy observer.

2   The Navy did not fly the practice flight profiles which were directed by the Pentagon. The helos were never tested to the degree the mission required. That alone was responsible for mission failure.

Chapter 8, Desert One to Abort

1   When Clem got back to the States, he personally delivered a copy of the newspaper to the JTF J-2's desk and demanded, "Who the hell is the idiot that tried to get us killed?" It is assumed the staff officer was quickly hidden from the team.
2   Fred Arooji remained, staying with family up country.
3   All the members of the force received the Humanitarian Service Medal. In addition, Stuart O'Neill received the Soldier's Medal for pulling an injured soldier from the wreckage of the C-130. Sergeants Lemke, McEwan, and Arooji also received the Defense Superior Service Medal for their activities in Tehran.

Chapter 10, The New Plan

1   Other than the three hostages at the MFA, planners could locate no more than three other hostages on a given day, as they were moved periodically.

Chapter 12, The Little Birds

1   Part of the 101st Airborne Division.
2   Originally called Task Force 158 when formed in 1980, the unit was later designated as TF-160, then 160th Aviation Battalion, and eventually grew to become the 160th Special Operations Aviation Regiment, known by their nickname of "the Night Stalkers," with the motto "Night Stalkers Don't Quit."
3   Rumors persisted throughout the mission planning that four British nurses were also held at the MFA. Possibly wishful thinking, but the unit was prepared to bring them out in addition to the three Americans.

Chapter 13, Florida

1   The lead birds for the first security team had no recognition stripes, the hostage recovery team's birds had a single stripe, and the second security team's birds were designated with two stripes.
2   Apparently, this was a known problem with the OH-6 because the pilots all laughed it off (nervously).

Chapter 14, It's All Over but the Shouting

1 There have been allegations of clandestine dealing between the Reagan campaign and Iran since. See: https://www.nytimes.com/2023/03/18/us/politics/jimmycarter-october-surprise-iran-hostages.html accessed April 1, 2023.

2 An additional factor for the cancellation was its compromise by journalist Jack Anderson. In the fall of 1981, Anderson announced the military was preparing for a second mission. His announcement may have alerted the Iranians as there were indications the mission would have met resistance.

Bibliography

Bottoms, Mike, "Eagle Claw veteran, Special Ops Aviator receives 2013 Bull Simons Award," article retrieved from USSOCOM website, at https://www.socom.mil/Pages/EagleClawveteranSpecialOpsAviatorreceives2013BullSimonsAward.aspx.

Carter, Jimmy, quoted in Rose McDermott, "The Iranian Hostage Rescue Mission," *Risk-Taking in International Politics: Prospect Theory in American Foreign Policy*, Ann Arbor: University of Michigan Press, 1998.

DODD (Department of Defense Documents), downloaded from: https://archive.org/details/IranianHostageRescueAttempt/Iranian%20Hostage%20Rescue%20Attempt%20Execution%20of%20Rescue%20Option%20and%20Training/page/n5/mode/2up, accessed September 20, 2020.

Dolan, Ronald E., *A History of the 160th Special Operations Aviation Regiment (Airborne)*. Washington, D.C.: Federal Research Division, Library of Congress, Oct. 2001.

Finlayson, Kenneth, "Desert One and Operation Eagle Claw," Interview with Col. Stanley Olchovik, *Special Forces: The First Fifty Years*, Tampa: Faircount LLC for the Special Forces Association, 2002.

Headquarters, Joint Task Force, COMJTF OPLAN: Rescue of American Hostages From AMEMB Iran, Washington, D.C.: HQJTF, February 26, 1980. Declassified.

Hoe, Alan, *The Quiet Professional: Major Richard J. Meadows of the U.S. Army Special Forces*, University Press of Kentucky: Lexington, 2011.

Kyle, James, *The Guts to Try: The Untold Story of the Iran Hostage Rescue Mission by the On-scene Desert Commander*, New York: Orion Crown, 1990.

Laingen, Bruce, "The Iran Hostage Crisis: Moments in U.S. Diplomatic History" [article online], available at http://adst.org/2012/10/the-iran-hostage-crisis-part-i/.

Lenahan, Rod, *Crippled Eagle: A Historical Perspective of U.S. Special Operations, 1976–1990*, Charleston: Narwal Press, 1998.

Pushies, Fred J., *Night Stalkers: 160th Special Operations Aviation Regiment (Airborne)*, St. Paul: Zenith Press, 2005.

Special Air Service, "Close Quarter Battle" [Unpublished training document], undated, circa 1975.

Stejskal, James, *Special Forces Berlin: Clandestine Cold War Operations of the US Army's Elite, 1956–1990*, Oxford: Casemate, 2016.

Index